# A
# CAPITALIST
# MANIFESTO

# A
# CAPITALIST
# MANIFESTO

### UNDERSTANDING THE MARKET
### ECONOMY AND DEFENDING LIBERTY

BY

# GARY WOLFRAM

## DG
DUNLAP GODDARD

Published in the United States of America.
Manufactured in the United States of America.

ISBN-13: 978-0-965-60403-1 (trade paperback: acid free)
ISBN-13: 978-0-965-60404-8 (ebook)
LCCN: 2012952249
A CIP catalogue record for this book is available from the publisher.

Jacket Design by Jeremy Bronson

QUANTITY PURCHASES: Companies, professional groups, clubs and other organizations may qualify for special terms when ordering quantities of this title. For information, email Special Sales Department at info@dunlap-goddard.com.

Economics is too important to be left to the experts.
—LUDWIG VON MISES

Our reliance is in the love of liberty which God has planted in our bosoms. Our defense is in the preservation of the spirit which prizes liberty as the heritage of all men, in all lands, everywhere.
—ABRAHAM LINCOLN

# CONTENTS

# Chapter I

# THE ROOTS OF CAPITALISM

THE ROOTS OF CAPITALISM are ancient, so ancient in fact that they likely predate even language in the development of civilization. Capitalism arose from something so uniquely human and so intuitive that it may well be hard wired into our genetic code—barter.

Imagine the dawn of man, clans of hunter-gatherers following the herds in search of food. A few of our ancestors doubtless possessed greater physical abilities and refined skills in hunting game or locating edible vegetation, and their success won them a greater share of the bounty. Even at this primitive stage, other members of the clan would have specialized in the making of tools or the tanning of hides, activities that support the primary goal of feeding the clan. Those earning a greater share of the bounty would exchange some of their perishable surplus for a straighter spear or warmer clothing—simple barter transactions based on the perceived value of the goods offered. Capitalism evolved as one of the earliest characteristics distinguishing human behavior from that of all other animals; we alone have developed the ability to satisfy our needs and wants through the peaceful exchange of value for value.

The elegant beauty of capitalism lies in the fact that regardless of how global or interconnected the world becomes economically, it never loses sight of the importance of the individual. The genius of capitalism is that it is not a monolithic, centrally planned monstrosity, but rather a fluid system with millions of individual exchanges, resulting in the most efficient allocation of resources. The difference between centrally planned economies and free market capitalism is the difference between glaciers and the ocean.

The debate over government's role in the economy is a staple of modern politics, with opposing sides arguing for greater or lesser intervention in the marketplace. This debate took on a new form in the fall of 2011 with the Occupy Wall Street protest. Interviews with these anticapitalism protesters reminded me of a scene in the 1979 Monty Python film *The Life of Brian* that ended with the following exchange between a group of anti-Roman protesters:

> PROTESTER 1: "All right...all right...but apart from better sanitation and medicine and education and irrigation and public health and roads and a fresh water system and baths and public order...what have the Romans done for us?"
> PROTESTER 2: "Brought peace!"
> PROTESTER 1: "What?! Oh...Peace, yes...shut up!"

In a similar vein, the Occupy Wall Street crowd's reactionary furor against capitalism apparently blinds them to the myriad benefits of capitalism, including many that have made both their lives and even their protest possible. In their demagoguery they conveniently ignore the fact that modern market capitalism has reduced poverty and raised life expectancy more in the past century than did all previous economic systems in the previous five thousand years of recorded human history.

The Wall Street protesters lack a fundamental understanding of capitalism and how the market system works. They appear to think that the cell phones they use, food they eat, hotels and tents they stay in, their sleeping bags and clothes, the cars they drive and the fuel that powers them and all the goods and services they consume every day would exist under a different system, perhaps in more abundance.

While the hypocrisy of the Occupy Wall Street crowd maybe entertaining, the threat they and their like-minded allies pose to civilization is real and rooted in a lack of understanding of the founding American principles of individual liberty and self-governance. We are threatened by an education system that fails to instruct our children in how limited government and a market economy lead to liberty and wealth for the masses.

The reason people in sub-Saharan Africa and rural India live like refugees is not that they don't work as hard as we do, or are not as smart as we are, but that they live in an economic system that doesn't allow them to be productive. The basis of our economic prosperity is market capitalism, individual liberty and responsibility, and limited government.

It took six thousand years from the invention of the wheel until we developed the two-wheel cart. In the film *The Ten Commandments*, we see Moses parting the Red Sea to let the Israelites escape from the Pharaoh's army, which is riding in two-wheeled carts. From the time of Moses to Wyatt Earp we move from two-wheeled carts to four-wheeled carts—buckboards and stagecoaches. Yet Wyatt Earp, who is an adult when he participates in the gunfight at the OK Corral, sees the movement from four-wheel carts to the Model T. My grandparents were born before man had ever seen powered flight, yet lived to see a time when you could buy a trip into space. The rapid increase in innovation and the wealth of the masses occurred because the West gradually developed the economic system of market capitalism and a compatible political system.

Capitalism allows for the creation the greatest wealth for the masses, and offers the greatest benefits and opportunities to the poor. Capitalism is not a collusion between big business and big government to advance the interests of stockholders and management at the expense of workers—it is rather a system of voluntary exchange based on private property rights, limited government, and individual freedom. Voluntary exchange ensures that only businesses that provide what consumers want at the right price will survive, fostering continuous innovation. One becomes wealthy in a market system by pleasing others, and the more individuals you please the wealthier you become.

Each day we go about our business in complete confidence that the rest of society will provide for our basic needs. Typically, we do not stop to wonder how food gets to our table, clothes into our closet, or how our shelter is provided. We do not take the time to consider that millions of people will awake in our largest cities tomorrow and there will be the right amount of coffee, dental floss, toilet paper, and an astonishing array of other goods and services sold during the day. Yet if we do stop to think about it, it is a miracle.

The market system delivers untold wealth to millions of persons. Societies that do not have market economies have been forced to concede that only free markets are capable of producing on a scale that affords even the poorest person a standard of living well above what would have been unthinkable just a few hundred years ago.

Socioeconomic order is determined by the rules under which we play the game. This is the political process. But as the French political economist Frédéric Bastiat noted, it is not possible to develop a science of politics without understanding how the economic system works. Nobel laureate Friedrich Hayek refined this idea by offering that if people do not understand and believe in market capitalism, they will ask their government to undertake actions that in the end will make us less wealthy and free. This has proven true with the faltering Western social democracies and lies at the root of anticapitalist movements.

What goes wrong in today's society too often occurs because people have not thought very much about how the world works. They are too busy, think themselves uninformed, or simply aren't interested. However, it does not require more than an ability to read and think critically to make sense of many confusing and contradictory statements; to recognize that what our government does to solve problems often makes things worse and that federal, state, and local officials are often advised that their policies will fail.

The difference between a good economist and a bad economist, Bastiat observed, is that the bad economist sees the seen, but the good economist sees the unforeseen. In other words, the good economist can imagine the unintended consequences of a policy action. The goal of this book is to make you a good economist.

# Chapter II

# TWO ECONOMISTS ON A BUS

THERE ARE A NUMBER of colleges and universities in Western Massachusetts. Years ago, five of these formed a compact to share facilities and to operate a bus service between their campuses. The buses are free to all students and are often taken between one of the all-women and one of the all-men colleges on Friday and Saturday evenings.

One evening, while riding this bus with a colleague, we were talking to two students about an incident that occurred the previous winter. We were told that one of the buses could not negotiate the steep hill that separates two colleges with a full load of passengers because of the snow. The bus driver needed to have ten students exit the bus in order to make it up the hill.

My colleague and I failed to sympathize with one of the students telling the story, who had to exit the bus and walk up the hill in a snowstorm. Instead, we were sidetracked with how to optimally choose ten persons to exit the bus.

There are, of course, a number of ways to pick the ten unfortunate students who must walk up the hill. Some of those that readily came to mind were:

1. Choose the last ten persons who boarded the bus, a sort of first-come, first-served solution;

2. Choose those who are best dressed for the inclement weather;

3. Choose those who appear to be in the best shape to make the walk up the hill;

4. Choose ten freshmen.

You can easily envision a number of other options. Most would involve some sense of fairness using a rule that has been established in other contexts, such as a seniority solution (#4), or attempting to judge who among the students would be least inconvenienced by having to walk (#3). The problem with solutions like these is that only those students on the bus can know to what extent they may be inconvenienced, or what special circumstances might make blindly following a rule of thumb unfair.

A solution that came immediately to my colleague and me was to have everyone exit the bus and then buy their way back on. This solution has some appealing characteristics. First, it does not require the bus driver or anyone in authority to judge which students would be best able to climb the hill. Neither does it force anyone to make the value judgment of which solution is most fair. Instead, it allows each individual to express his or her value of remaining on the bus. Special circumstances can be taken into account, and students can express their intensity of preference by the amount they are willing to pay to get back on the bus.

Second, there exists a price at which exactly ten persons will be unwilling to pay to get back on the bus. If the bus driver sets the price at $2 and all but two want to ride the bus, he can move the price higher. If at $4 there are too few riders, he can move the price lower. There will be a price at which the quantity of seats available will equal the amount of seats demanded.

This market-type solution brings up a number of questions. First, what might one do with the money earned from selling the bus seats? In this case, it really doesn't matter where the money goes.[1] Let's suppose for now that the money is divided among the ten students who did not ride the bus. This would compensate them for their misfortune and might seem like the right thing to do.

Another obvious question: what does one do about those students who forgot to bring their money?[2] It may not seem fair that some students do not have any money with them and therefore cannot express their intensity of preference as well as those who have brought their wallets.

One solution is an impromptu capital market where people can borrow from each other. Some students will give up some of their current purchasing power in order to receive the money at a later date. Being friends, and supposing that they will all be back at their dorms later to settle their accounts, the students might simply loan the money to one another at no cost. But it may be that some students would be willing to loan their money only if compensated by receiving interest, thus being ensured that they will be able to purchase more in the future with the money they are lending today. In any event, the failure to bring money need not consign a student to walking up the hill. Nonetheless, some may be bothered by the fact that the wealthier students have a better chance of remaining on the bus.

Let us go back to the suggestion that the seats be chosen by lottery. This seems fair enough; it means everyone has an equal chance of getting back on the bus. People who forgot their wallets might still be able to avoid the inconvenience of walking. However, there is one slight problem with this solution in that it does not go far enough: people should be able to trade their lottery chances either before or after the drawing. This would allow gains from trade to be realized. The market process normally allows trading to occur whenever two persons feel they can improve their position through mutual exchange.

In this case, suppose you really would like to avoid walking, and though I don't prefer to walk, it is really of no great consequence to me either way. Under the pure lottery scheme, it is possible that I could get a seat on the bus, and that you might not be as lucky and have to walk.

Given how much money we have, there is a certain value each of us places on our chance of riding the bus. If you value that chance more than I do, there could be an improvement in both our situations if we can trade. Suppose I value my chance of getting a seat at $2, and you value a chance of winning a seat at $3. You could then offer me $2.50 for my chance, and I would accept. You would be better off because you would now possess an additional chance at getting the seat (which you valued at $3) for only $2.50. I too would be better off because I have given up my chance, which I valued at $2, and for which you have given me $2.50 in return. This illustrates that in the market process, exchange will occur whenever two people value a good differently and when both will benefit from the exchange.

We get similar results if we wait for the outcome of the lottery and then allow persons to sell their seats on the bus. The difference now, however, is that the price of the actual seat must be higher than the price of the chance for a seat. This is because we will always pay less for a mere chance than for the object itself.[3] In either case, free market exchange allows everyone the opportunity to improve his or her position.

# ENDNOTES

1. The purpose of the price in this case is simply to allocate the existing resource—the supply of bus seats, which is fixed. We will see later that one of the purposes of profit is to increase the amount of resources for the production of a good.
2. This question is related to the income distribution problem, which we will discuss later when examining incomes in a market economy.
3. An economist would say that the value of a chance for something is its "expected value." That is, the value multiplied by the probability that it will be obtained. For example, if the value of the seat is $2, but the chance is only 50 percent that you will get it, then the value of the chance is $2 x 50 percent, which equals $1. This is the expected value of the chance of the seat.

# Chapter III

# DEMAND

IN ROALD DAHL'S NOVEL *Charlie and the Chocolate Factory*, the horribly spoiled Veruca Salt distills the essence of unrestrained demand, screaming: "I want it all, and I want it now!" While like Veruca, we all have needs and wants, most of ours are tempered by the question, What are they worth to us?

## INDIVIDUAL BEHAVIOR

A DISTINCTIVE CHARACTERISTIC IN the field of economics is its focus on the individual. Other social scientists, sociologists for example, often examine the characteristics of groups and use group behavior to explain or predict individual behavior. Economists, on the other hand, do the opposite. They use information gathered from the study of individual behavior to discuss the behavior of entire groups.

Examining criminal behavior is a good example. One method of looking at such behavior starts with criminals as a group. We could try to find criminal characteristics, such as age, educational level, family status as children and adults, race, and psychological profiles. Then we would draw inferences from these characteristics and try to change criminals as a group.

Suppose we find that 60 percent of convicted robbers are twenty-five-year-old urban males with an eighth-grade education who have been convicted of a crime before the age of fifteen, come from a single-parent family, and are unmarried. From all of this information, we might try to explain how each of these characteristics contributes to criminal activity, and then initiate policies to reduce crime. For example, we might reduce the number of persons in the group by increasing the educational level of urban males.

Economists instead use theories of individual behavior to draw conclusions about what sorts of policies would be effective in reducing crime.

Most economic theory begins with the assumption that the best model of how the world works rests on the idea of a rational, self-interested individual who acts purposefully to achieve the highest level of satisfaction possible while operating under certain constraints.

Logicians define rationality as consistent thinking. Economists take a different approach. We define rationality as "choosing the option that one believes will increase his satisfaction the most when presented with a constrained choice."

We now have a definition of rationality, but what do we mean by self-interest? By self-interest we do not mean selfishness. We mean that people will make choices to improve their lives. This can come from buying a new shirt or by giving away the shirt off one's back. In a market economy people act to improve their well-being, not necessarily their wealth or number of possessions.

If we assume that individuals are rational and self-interested, then we can think of a simple rule that will lead us to maximize our satisfaction given any option. That rule is to compare the added benefits from an action to the added costs. If the added benefits exceed the added costs, then we undertake the action.[1] It will always be the case that if the added benefit from the action exceeds the added cost, I will have improved my position by doing it, and if the added cost exceeds the added benefit, I will reduce my total satisfaction.

Let us go back to our example of criminal activity. An economist would look at a criminal and say that if she commits a crime it is because she has made a rational choice. She weighed the added benefits from the crime against the added costs and determined that the added benefits exceeded the added costs. The practical implication of this with regards to public policy is that if we want to reduce criminal activity, we must reduce the benefit of committing a crime and increase its cost.

This might lead the same policy prescriptions of a sociologist reasoning from group to individual behavior. For example, an obvious cost of criminal activity is the chance of being caught and convicted. If this were to happen, one's future job prospects would be reduced. But if a person is in an area with high unemployment rates, and lacks even a high school education, the chances of finding a good job are pretty slim anyway. This is the case with our hypothetical criminal. Because there is little chance of her getting a good job, the loss of future job prospects will not be an effective deterrent. If we increase her education level and improve her job prospects, then the loss of these prospects due to a criminal record is greater; the cost of being convicted of any crime and going to prison has gone up, and she will be less likely to commit crime. We will have the same policy as our sociologist friend, but for different reasons.

Notice that convincing criminals to adopt an improved morality that avoids criminal activity is consistent with this line of thinking. By providing criminals with a better moral sense of right and wrong, we will also alter benefits and costs. An economist would simply say that criminals are behaving rationally because feelings of guilt are a cost that now must be weighed against the benefits of criminal activity.

## MARGINAL ANALYSIS

WE HAVE OBSERVED THAT rational individuals will continue any activity as long as the added benefits are greater than the added costs. How do we know this is true? Through marginal analysis—a concept economists developed in the latter part of the nineteenth century.

Economists had long been stumped by the diamond-water paradox. Why is it that diamonds, which are not necessary to sustain life, are expensive, while water, which is absolutely necessary, is relatively inexpensive? In the later part of the nineteenth century, Carl Menger in Austria, William Stanley Jevons in England, and Léon Walras in France independently came across the answer.[2] When three economists agree we know we are on to something.

While water is indeed necessary for survival, the value to consumers of the next glass or bottle of water is relatively small, as they generally have an abundance of water. However, since diamonds are far less abundant than water, the value of a diamond will always be higher.

Economists use the term "marginal" quite frequently and simply mean the next or last unit "at the margin." The insight of economists is that as long as the marginal benefit exceeds the marginal cost, we will continue an activity until the marginal benefit declines to the point where it equals the marginal cost. After that point we will reduce any activity.

While it is fun to come up with examples of where the diminishing marginal benefit rule, or "Law of Diminishing Returns," does not hold (romantic dinners with my wife), it is generally the case that the marginal benefit of anything declines as you do it more often or get more of it. This can be shown in a simple diagram, as in Figure 3-1.

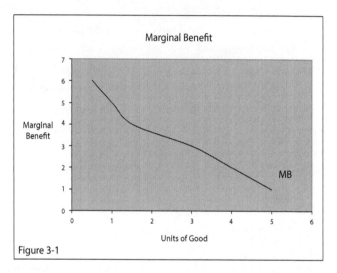

Figure 3-1

Economists also assume that the added cost of doing anything increases the more you do it after some point (marginal costs increases). There are other technical reasons why this should occur, but for our purposes we shall assume for the moment that after some point marginal costs will increase. This is shown in Figure 3-2.

In Figure 3-3, we show both the marginal benefits and marginal costs of eating oranges. The net benefit from, say, eating the fifth orange, is the difference between the marginal benefit curve and the marginal cost curve. This is shown for the fifth orange as the difference between points a and b in Figure 3-3.

As long as the marginal benefit curve lies above the marginal cost curve, additional oranges add to the total net benefit of eating oranges. Total net benefit is the area above the marginal cost curve and below the marginal benefit curve. It should be obvious that this area is maximized at the point where marginal benefit equals marginal cost. Past point c, where marginal benefit equals marginal cost (at seven oranges), you would be adding more to your cost than to your benefit. The net benefit of the eighth orange would be negative, thus lowering your total net benefit. Notice that marginal benefits can actually be negative; after a tenth orange additional oranges make you worse off. When you are "full" it means that eating an additional orange will make you less happy.

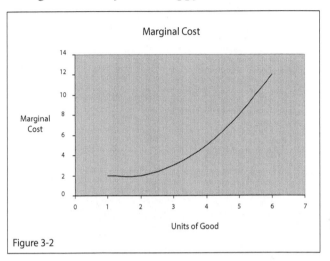

Figure 3-2

We will use this idea of individuals acting according to rational self-interest to examine the market process in terms of supply and demand. The famous British economist Alfred Marshall analyzed the market process by

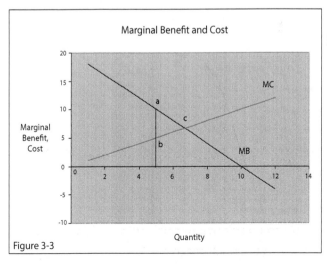

Figure 3-3

looking at demand and supply as two blades of a pair of scissors. Neither the demand for a product nor the supply of a product by itself determines how much of that product will be produced or at what price. One has to look at both demand and supply and how they interact. We will do this by first examining demand, then supply, and then how they interact to form market equilibrium.

## INDIVIDUAL DEMAND

THE DEMAND OF ANY individual for a good or service is a schedule of how much he would be willing to purchase at various prices. We can think of the situation where an auctioneer surveys you and asks how many pairs of shoes you would be willing to purchase if the price of each pair were $90, $85, $80, and so on. By listing the prices and the amount you would be willing to purchase, we would generate your demand for shoes.

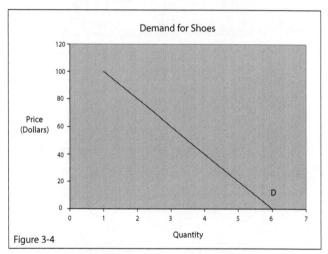

Figure 3-4

If we were to draw a picture of this relationship, it would look like Figure 3-4:

There are a few things we should notice right away. First, the demand is given at—and for—a certain point in time. We might ask how many pairs a week you would buy, how many pairs a year, how many pairs a decade, etc. Thus we would have to make a distinction between short-run and long run demand for shoes.

We also must be careful to distinguish between "demand" and "quantity demanded." Demand refers to the entire schedule of prices and quantities that the individual would be willing to purchase at those prices. In terms of the graph, it is the entire demand curve. Quantity demanded is how much an individual is willing to purchase at a particular price. Notice that changing the price does not change the demand curve; changing the price changes quantity demanded.

This is a mistake often made in the media. You will hear in a news story that the price of oil is rising and therefore demand is falling. This demonstrates that the news commentator does not understand the concept of market demand very well. If the price of oil rises, the demand for oil remains the same, but the quantity demanded of oil falls.

So what changes demand? Variables we have held constant when we surveyed our consumer and asked him how much of a good he would be willing to buy at various prices. These variables include preferences or tastes, an individual's income, and the prices of other goods, notably substitute and complementary goods.

People's preferences influence the demand curve. Economists normally take the preferences of the individual as given when examining demand. Of course, an entire industry is made up of folks who attempt to change your preferences. Advertising is a good example. You are told that a certain automobile will get you a date, or make you seem younger, or that a certain beer is less filling than any other beer. This type of advertising attempts to make you willing to purchase more of the product at the same price. In terms of our diagram, it means that at every price, you are willing to buy

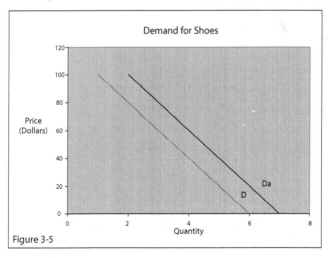

Figure 3-5

more beer than you were before watching the advertisement. This is shown by shifting the demand curve to the right, as from D to Da in Figure 3-5.

A second variable affecting demand is an individual's income. Each individual tries to maximize satisfaction given certain constraints. While there are a number of constraints for each of us—our time, our ability to per-form certain physical activities, etc.—in the simplest model, the constraint is income. Each of us has a limited amount of income, usually expressed in terms of money. Given the amount of money we have, we go out and make our purchases. The more money we have, the more purchases we can make and the greater amount of satisfaction we can obtain. If we are altruistic, we may use some of our income to gain satisfaction by giving money to our friends or to certain charities. In any event, the amount of a typical good or service we are willing to purchase at a given price will increase or decrease as our income rises based on whether the good is what economists call a "normal good" or an "inferior good."

Normal goods are defined as goods that we demand more of as our income rises. For example, we demand more housing services as our income rises. We thus find wealthier people purchasing greater amounts of housing services than poor people, especially in the form of larger, fancier homes. Many goods and services have the characteristic that, given a particular price for the good, we would purchase more of it if we had more income.

An inferior good is a good that we purchase less of as our income rises. This usually occurs because we stop buying the good in question, or reduce our consumption of it, and use another good. For example, hot dogs could be an inferior good for an individual. Suppose you earn $300 month as a paid intern. You might find yourself purchasing a lot of hot dogs given your budget constraint. Then you get a regular job that pays $900 per month. Even though your taste for hot dogs has not changed, if we find that you purchase fewer hot dogs when your income goes up, then hot dogs are an inferior good for you. In our diagram this would be shown by a shift in your demand curve to the left, as from D to Da in Figure 3-6. Notice a shift to the left means that at each price you would purchase fewer hot dogs than you would before your income rose.

The third thing affecting the demand curve is the price of substitutes. If you were asked how many cans of applesauce you would be willing to buy at various prices, your answer would surely depend on the price of

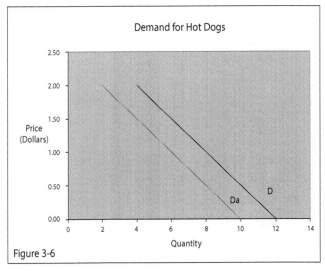

Figure 3-6

canned peaches or whatever other item you might eat instead. Suppose we have mapped out your demand for canned applesauce, and then the price of canned peaches falls from $0.70 to $0.40. Unless you can't stand canned peaches, you would probably change your answers to the questions about how many cans of applesauce you would purchase at the various prices. It would be reasonable to find that you buy less applesauce than you would have before the price of peaches dropped. Of course, this is precisely what the sellers of canned peaches hope for when they lower their price. You are

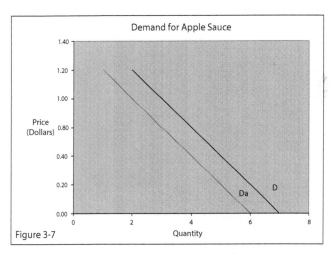

Figure 3-7

wandering down the aisle and put the applesauce in your cart. When you notice that there is a sale on peaches, you throw a few cans of peaches in your cart and take out the applesauce.

Figure 3-7 shows the situation of substitutes affecting demand. Suppose the price of peaches falls from $0.70 to $0.40. You will buy more peaches than before, but you will now buy fewer cans of applesauce at every price of applesauce, since apple sauce and peaches are substitutes. The fall in the price of peaches causes your demand for applesauce to shift to the left. This is shown in Figure 3-7.

The fourth and final category of those things affecting the demand curve is complements. Two goods are complements if when the price of one of the goods rises, the demand for the other good falls. Goods are also called complements if when the price of one good falls, the demand for the other good increases. Going back to our hot dog example, hot dogs and hot dog buns might be two such goods. Suppose we determine your demand for hot dog buns. You would be willing to buy three packages a week at $1 a package, four packages a week at $0.75 a package, five packages at $0.50 a package, and so on. This is represented by D in Figure 3-8. Now suppose the price of hot dogs rises from $1.25 to $3.50 per package. This moves you up your demand curve for hot dogs, decreasing the quantity demanded of hot dogs. But now that you are buying fewer hot dogs, you will want to buy fewer hot dog buns. Thus, at every price for hot dog buns we will find that you want to buy fewer hot dog buns than you did before the price of hot dogs changed. Your demand for hot dog buns has declined, and the demand

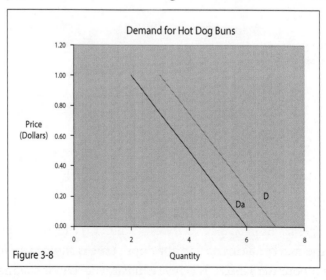

Figure 3-8

curve shifts to the left. This effect of the price of a good (in this case, hot dogs) on the demand for its complement (hot dog buns) is represented in Figure 3-8 by a shift in demand from D to Da.

To summarize what has been said so far: The demand of an individual for a product is how much that individual would be willing to buy of that product at various prices. The quantity demanded increases as the price falls, so that the demand curve, which graphically shows the individual demand, slopes down. Each individual's demand curve depends on an individual's tastes for goods, income, and the prices of other goods, in particular, prices of substitutes and complements. Changes in any of these causes the demand to change, represented by the demand curve shifting to the left or right.[3]

## MARKET DEMAND

THE MARKET DEMAND CURVE for any product is the sum of the demand curves of all the individuals in that market. If you and I are the only ones in the market, and you would purchase four packages of hot dogs at $1.25 and I would purchase three packages at that price, then one point on the market demand curve for hot dogs would be the price $1.25 with quantity

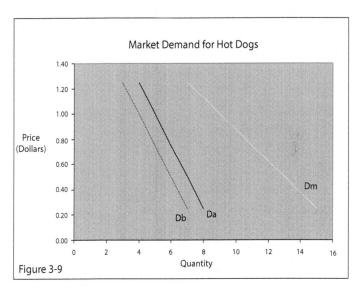

Figure 3-9

demanded of seven packages. We would then do this for all prices and generate the market demand for hot dogs. This is shown in Figure 3-9, where Da is your demand, Db is my demand, and Dm is the market demand.

Market demand curves have all the characteristics of individual demand curves. That is, they slope down and depend upon tastes, income, and the prices of substitutes and complements.

The market demand curve does not by itself tell us what the price will be in the market, or what the market price will tend toward (neither does the individual demand curve). We must add the concept of market supply, which we do in chapter 4. In chapter 5 we will examine how market demand interacts with market supply to determine prices and quantities sold in a market. But first we will introduce the concept of elasticity.

## ELASTICITY

I WAS INTRODUCED TO the concept of elasticity as an undergraduate. While it made sense to me mathematically, I did not see much use for it. I just memorized the formula, answered an exam question about it, and promptly forgot it. Then in my advanced undergraduate and graduate courses, elasticity appeared to be more of a mathematical trick than a practical idea. It wasn't until I became an adviser to the Michigan State Senate that I saw how often the concept of elasticity is important in public policy.

We just noted several times that demand curves slope down because when prices fall, the quantity demanded increases (and vice versa). But an important question about the demand for a product is How much does quantity demanded rise when the price falls? For example, if I am a state senator and vote for a bill that would impose a 4 percent tax on the price of hot dogs, and this causes hot dog prices to rise by 3 percent, I know that the quantity demanded of hot dogs will go down. But if I have a major hot dog supplier in my district it will be important for me to know whether hot dog sales will go down by only one-half of a percent or by 15 percent. If I know the price elasticity of demand for hot dogs, I can answer this question.

We think of something as being elastic if when a force is applied to it, it responds significantly, and inelastic if it doesn't respond at all. Price elasticity of demand reflects this general idea of elasticity.

When determining whether the demand for hot dogs is elastic or inelastic, we need to know if the percentage change in quantity demanded following a price change is bigger or smaller than the percentage change in the price. If the percentage change in quantity demanded is larger than the percentage change in price, we say that in this portion of the demand curve for hot dogs the price is elastic. On the other hand, if the percentage change in quantity demanded is smaller than the percentage change in price, we say the demand is inelastic.

One of the most useful pieces of information that price elasticity of demand tells us is what happens to the total amount of money spent on a good when the price changes. Total revenue is defined as the price of the good times the quantity sold. If you are the seller of a good, then your total revenue is price times the amount you sold. Thus, if hot dogs are $1.25 per package, and ten packages are sold at this price, total revenue is $12.50. Total expenditure is the same thing, only from a different perspective. If you are the purchaser of a good, then total expenditure is the price of the good times the amount that you bought. Total expenditure and total revenue are both defined as price times quantity.

We know that whenever we raise the price of a good the quantity demanded falls. If quantity demanded goes down as price goes up, what happens to total expenditures when price goes up? Recall that price elasticity tells you how much quantity demanded goes down when price goes up. If the demand is inelastic, we know that the percentage change in quantity demanded will be less than the percentage change in price. Thus, for the case of a good with inelastic demand, if the price rises, total expenditure on the good will increase. The increase in price is not fully offset by a decrease in quantity demanded. In other words, price is rising faster than the quantity demanded is falling, and total expenditure (price times quantity) goes up. Just the opposite occurs if the demand is elastic: the quantity demanded falls faster than the price rises, and total expenditure falls.

Let's put these ideas of elasticity and total expenditure to practical use. Suppose you are the staff director for a Senate committee that deals with federal drug policy. You are told that the chairman of the committee, Senator Czar, is considering a bill that would, if it became law, have the effect of increasing the price of crack cocaine in the United States. Senator Czar calls you into her office and asks your opinion of the effectiveness of such legislation in dealing with the nation's cocaine problem.

Since you know how elasticity works, you could apply this concept in answering. You could first look at the price elasticity of demand for crack cocaine. You might try to estimate it by gathering data on prices and quantity demanded, or you might review some articles written about cocaine that have estimates in them. Even if you do not have an exact number, you can make an educated guess whether it is elastic or inelastic. This would entail thinking about whether the quantity demanded changes in percentage terms as much as the price changes.

It is generally acknowledged that crack cocaine is addictive. It is therefore probably true that people who use crack cocaine would not be able to reduce their consumption of it much if the price were to go up (supposing there is no substitute). We would expect that a rise in the price of cocaine of 10 percent would result in less than a 10 percent decline in cocaine purchased by the average crack cocaine user. This means that the individual demand for cocaine is inelastic.

The next logical step is to think about market demand in terms of elasticity. Since we have already determined that people who are addicted to cocaine are not likely to have elastic demand, it is therefore a relatively good assumption that the market demand for crack cocaine is also inelastic. Remember: the market demand for cocaine is the sum of individual demands.

Having now come to this conclusion, you explain this to Senator Czar. If the senator wishes to reduce the quantity of crack cocaine demanded, then increasing the price of cocaine will accomplish that. How much the quantity demanded goes down depends upon the price elasticity. Having just explained that the demand for cocaine is inelastic, you can advise her not to expect a large drop in the quantity demanded of cocaine unless her policy will have a substantial effect on the price.

But you can offer her additional information. If the demand for cocaine is inelastic, then increasing its price will cause total expenditures on cocaine to go up. This means that the people who use cocaine will spend more of their income on cocaine, and total revenue for those who sell cocaine will increase. If the senator wishes to reduce total expenditures on cocaine, rather than reduce quantity demanded, then the bill will do just the opposite of what she wishes. If, say, theft is related to how much people spend on cocaine because cocaine addicts must steal to sustain their habit, then her policy would increase crime.

Using the simple concept of elasticity, you can alert Senator Czar to the fact that the bill, while it may appear to be good public policy at first, will actually cause greater expenditures on cocaine, greater revenue for cocaine dealers, and more crime, to the extent that theft is related to drug use.

There are two important elements to elasticity that warrant further discussion. First, elasticity is defined at a given point along the demand curve. It is possible for elasticity to be different at every point along a demand curve, or to be the same at every point. In fact, a demand curve that is a straight line has the characteristic that, while its slope is constant, elasticity differs at every point. Thus, when discussing whether demand is inelastic or elastic, we usually speak of it as being "elastic in the relevant range," or "inelastic in the relevant range." This means that in the area of the curve under discussion, the elasticity is elastic or inelastic.

It is also important to note that demand curves are more elastic the longer the time is that individuals have to respond to a price change. For example, if the price of gasoline doubled, in the short run you would probably not reduce your gasoline consumption by one-half. However, over the course of a year or two you might buy a car that gets better gas mileage or even move closer to work. So long run demand curves are generally more elastic than short run demand curves.

Why should you care about concepts such as elasticity? You might not be an adviser to a U.S. senator, but you are a citizen and probably a taxpayer. If citizens are not able to judge for themselves the policies and opinions of politicians, bureaucrats, and the media, then government policies may produce exactly the opposite of what citizens need or want.

## ENDNOTES

1. This will be discussed in greater detail under marginal benefits and marginal costs, but for now this may be accepted as a general rule.
2. For those interested in the history of economic thought, see William Stanley Jevons, "Brief Account of a General Mathematical Theory of Political Economy," Journal of the Royal Statistical Society, 29 June 1866, 282-87; Carl Menger, Principles of Economics, originally published in 1871 and available online from the Ludwig von Mises Institute at http://www.mises.org/etexts/menger/principles.asp; and Leon Walras, Éléments d'Économie Politique Pure, Ou, Théorie de la Richesse Sociale, originally published in 1874 by L. Corbaz & cie., available online at http://archive.org/stream/lmentsdconomiep00walrgoog#page/n13/mode/2up.
3. The slopes of the curves may change as well, although the demand curve will always slope down and the supply curve will always slope up.

# Chapter IV

# SUPPLY

DEMAND IS AN EMPTY space that supply strives to fill. In the 1994 film *The Shawshank Redemption*, Ellis "Red" Redding describes his role in the prison's black market: "There's a con like me in every prison in America, I guess. I'm the guy who can get it for you. Cigarettes, a bag of reefer if you're partial, a bottle of brandy to celebrate your kid's high school graduation. Damn near anything, within reason."

## OPPORTUNITY COST

SUPPOSE YOU ARE AT a party and have been there for three hours but now you have to get back to studying. Then the party host announces that free pizzas are arriving. What the host really means is that he is not going to charge you for the pizza. But are they really free to you? Most people would say yes and think no further. There is, however, a cost to you for staying and eating, and that cost is the value of whatever else you would be doing with your time if you did not stay to eat pizza.

If you valued studying for your exam at $3 per hour, and you would take an hour to eat and mingle (you would not want to shoot out of the party seconds after devouring the last piece of pizza and risk not getting invited back), then the pizza really costs you $3. An economist would say that the opportunity cost of the pizza is the $3 value you placed on the time you would have spent somewhere else.

Opportunity cost is defined more generally as whatever you must give up in order to get something. It is the value of your next-best opportunity, and that is why it is called opportunity cost. Individuals often have an innate sense of opportunity cost and make rational choices based on it. But sometimes they do not. Government policies, for example, are often made to sound beneficial when really they are not if you take opportunity cost into account.

As indicated in our free pizza situation, people often overlook the opportunity cost of their time. When deciding whether or not to spend four years at college, one usually considers the cost of tuition, books, room and board, and other out-of-pocket expenses. But one should also consider the opportunity cost of your time. If you could earn $20 per hour in an automobile factory straight out of high school, then in addition to the other expenses, the opportunity cost of a year of college would include what you could have earned in the automobile factory. Since there are about two thousand hours in a work year, you would be giving up $40,000 per year to attend college.

Now you might earn some money during the summer of your school year. Nonetheless, the opportunity cost of going to school would still be considerable. It would not be surprising to discover that a large number of highly paid factory workers did not go to college. It wouldn't necessarily be that they were uninterested in higher education or did not have the grades to get into college. It is simply the case that the opportunity cost of college was higher for them than for teenagers who did not have such job opportunities available to them.

This also explains why certain outstanding college football and basketball players do not complete college. They are able to earn sufficiently high salaries in professional sports such that the opportunity cost of finishing their education is too high. If we remember the old expression "I had something better to do," we can remember that we should always examine the opportunity cost of our time when making a decision.

Let's apply the idea of opportunity cost to public policy. Public officials often do not include the opportunity cost of our tax dollars when espousing the benefits of a program. Suppose that Representative Pacbucks has a program that funds early childhood education. This program will cost $50 million in tax dollars. The representative explains all the good aspects of the program and says that it will solve a number of pressing social problems. But even if the program is effective in solving some of these social problems, we still do not know if we should support it until we also know the other uses for the $50 million. For example, by spending $50 million on the early childhood program we cannot spend the same $50 million on prenatal care for the poor or on a new hospital for cancer patients. We must also think about what the $50 million could do if it remained in the pockets of taxpayers who might buy more milk for their children, or purchase more housing services.

The economist Henry Hazlitt pointed out more than fifty years ago that when government undertakes a project, such as building a bridge, the project is visible and can be appreciated.[1] What is not seen is the opportunity cost of the project, those items that were not built because the resources that went into the bridge were diverted from other uses. The point is that resources used for one thing cannot be used for something else. It is important to recognize these forgone opportunities.

## OBTAINING RESOURCES

IN ORDER TO GET the resources to produce something in a market economy you must bid those resources away from whatever else they might be used for. This applies to nonhuman resources, such as cement and steel, and to human labor services as well. In the terminology introduced above, you must pay the resource owner his opportunity cost.

If I own ten tons of steel and you wish to use that steel to build an apartment complex, then you must pay me at least as much for my steel as I can get from anyone else who also wishes to buy it. This is also true of labor services. If I can earn $8 per hour at the local car wash, and you wish to have me work in your restaurant, the opportunity cost of working for you is the $8 per hour I could earn at the car wash. You must pay me at least $8 per hour to work at your restaurant.

Persons who supply goods and services to the economy must therefore pay the owner of the resource the opportunity cost of that resource to obtain it for the production process. However, they cannot pay more for a resource than the value of the added product that results from using that resource. If they did, they would not survive long in a market economy. For example, if you were to hire me at $8 per hour, and I produced only $4 per hour worth of services, then you would either have to lower my wage, fire me, or go out of business.

There are two results from this phenomenon of having to pay the opportunity costs of resources. First, we know that in a market economy resources are put to their most valued use since owners of a resource can freely sell the resource to the highest bidder. If you offer me $10 per ton for my steel, you must be getting at least $10 per ton of product out of it; otherwise you'd go out of business. If you are the highest bidder for my steel, I will sell it to you and it could have had no higher valued use in society. If it did, someone would have bid more than the $10.

Second, consumers determine the value of resources and thus the income of resource owners (this includes the wages of individuals). This is because producers cannot pay a resource owner more than the amount that consumers value the added product or service that results from the use of any resource. For example, if you are a buggy whip maker, and I hire you to make buggy whips in my factory, and consumers decide they no longer want to purchase buggy whips, I cannot continue to hire you at the wage we originally agreed on. The lack of consumer demand for the product that you produce and I sell will lower both our incomes. This, of course, is true for all resources and their owners. As soon as consumers reduce their demand for a good or service, the earnings of all resources in that industry will decline. Likewise, when consumers increase their demand for a product, the earnings of all resource owners in that industry will increase.

As another example, suppose I were paying you $10 per hour to work in my buggy whip factory, and by hiring you the company would be making five more buggy whips per hour. If the price of buggy whips were $3, it would make sense for me to hire you, since I would be taking in an extra $15 per hour. However, if the price of buggy whips fell to $1, then I would be paying you $10 per hour and I would only be taking in an extra $5 per hour for your work. It would not take long for me to go out of business under such circumstances. The only way for me to be able to continue employing you would be for your wage to fall or for you to work more productively so that you were adding as much to my revenue as your wages were costing me.

## SUPPLY CURVE

HAVING LOOKED AT THE ideas of opportunity cost and obtaining resources, we can now use the same concepts for supply that we did for demand. We can imagine an auctioneer asking producers of a particular good how many units they would be willing to produce at various prices. We could then create a supply curve in the same way we fashioned a demand curve. Pick a given price and see how many units would be offered for sale, pick another price and see how many units would be offered, and continue over a wide range of prices. What would the shape of the supply curve look like?

First, it would slope upward because in order to produce more of a good I must obtain more resources. As my fellow producers and I try to get more of a resource, say steel, we will have to obtain it from resource owners who have higher and higher opportunity costs. In order to get the first ton of steel we may get it from a small dealer in town who doesn't have many places to market his steel. But as we try to get more and more, we may have to get some from producers who have been offered high prices from the auto industry. Or think of trying to get a babysitter on New Year's Eve. If you need one babysitter, you might be able to find someone who doesn't have a boyfriend, has no hope of getting a date, and would be just as willing to watch your TV as their own. But if you need ten babysitters, you might have to pay someone who would be giving up a splendid night on the town that they value at $100.

Using our general rule that we continue to do things as long as the marginal benefit exceeds the marginal cost, I will continue to produce more of a good as long as the marginal cost is less than the price. This means that the supply curve for a firm will be its marginal cost curve. Since marginal cost rises as the number of units of the output rises, at least after some point, the firm's supply curve will slope upwards, as in Figure 4-1.

Here we have the market supply curve for telephones. At $20 per phone, producers would supply fifty phones; at $40 they would supply seventy-five phones, and so on.

Just as with demand, we want to be careful of the difference between "supply" and "quantity supplied." Supply refers to the whole schedule or curve, whereas quantity supplied is the amount that would be offered at a particular price. Thus there is a quantity supplied for each price, and the entire set of prices and quantities supplied is referred to as supply.

As we did with demand curves, we need to examine what affects the supply curve, namely the price of inputs, technology, and the number of producers. The first major determinant of supply is the price of inputs. Inputs are those resources that go into the production of any given prod-

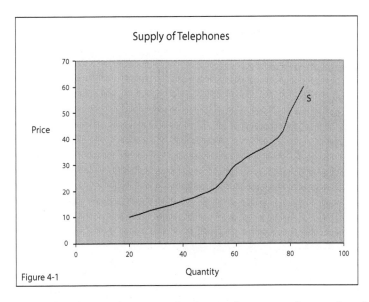

Figure 4-1

uct. Recall that the demand curve only shows the price of a good and the quantity demanded. Anything else that affects the demand for a good other than price is shown by a shift in the demand curve. The same holds true for the supply curve. Our next logical question, then, is, How do inputs affect the supply curve?

As we noted when thinking about why supply curves slope up, an important determinant of how much of any given good will be offered to the market at any given price is the price of resources used to produce the good. For example, since oil is used to produce gasoline, if the price of oil goes from $25 per barrel to $40 per barrel, then the amount of gasoline that a producer is willing to sell at each price (and willing to produce) will surely be less than before the price increase. A general rule can be stated here: as the price of an input goes up, producers are willing to produce less of a product at every price, and thus the supply curve for the product containing that input shifts left. This is indicated by a shift of the supply curve from S to S′ in Figure 4-2.

At oil prices of $25 per barrel, gasoline producers were willing to sell 1,200 gallons at $1.25, 1,000 gallons at $1 per gallon, 900 gallons at $0.90 per gallon, etc. This is indicated by supply curve S. When the price of oil rises to $40 per barrel, then producers of gasoline will only offer 1,000 gallons at $1.25 per gallon, 800 gallons at $1, and 600 gallons at $0.90. This is shown in Figure 4-2 by shifting the supply curve to S′.

If the price of an input fell—perhaps if oil went to $20 per barrel in our example—then the supply curve for gasoline would shift to the right. At every price producers would be willing to supply more than before the fall in the price of the input.

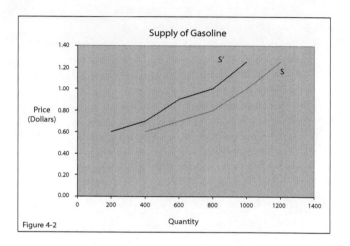

Figure 4-2

Another primary determinant of supply is the technology of production. Technology of production determines how much of the output can be produced for a given input. One of the major changes that occurred during the Industrial Revolution involved techniques of production that allowed goods to be produced at substantially lower cost than had been previously possible. When the production techniques change so a good can be produced at lower cost (often by using cheaper or fewer inputs for the same output), then we would expect producers to be willing to supply more of a good at any given price. Again, this is seen as a shift in the supply curve to the right.

The third major determinant of supply is the number of producers in the market. When our hypothetical auctioneer was asking how much would be produced at a given price, he was asking the question of a fixed number of producers. But suppose the number of producers in the market increased. Then, of course, for each price we would get a larger quantity supplied. This is shown by a shift in the supply curve to the right. If the number of producers in the market declined, the quantity supplied at each price would decline and would be shown by a shift in the supply curve to the left.

# ENDNOTES

1. See his classic, Economics in One Lesson (New York: Arlington House, 1979), originally published by Harper and Bros. in 1946

# Chapter V

# EQUILIBRIUM

NOW WE HAVE THE basic tools of demand and supply at our disposal. By putting the two curves together, we can get an idea what the market price and quantity will be.

## PUTTING DEMAND AND SUPPLY TOGETHER

FIGURE 5-1 ILLUSTRATES DEMAND and supply curves. Notice the demand curve slopes down and the supply curve slopes up. This means that as prices fall a greater quantity is demanded and a smaller quantity is supplied. Notice also that there is one point where the demand and supply curves intersect.

Suppose that this is the demand and supply of tractor caps. At $5 we see that the quantity demanded of tractor caps is 800, and that the quantity supplied of tractor caps is 800. There are no people out there who want tractor caps for $5 that can't find them, and there are no producers who have a big stock of tractor caps sitting around that they had hoped to sell for $5. This is what economists call market equilibrium.

Suppose we look at the $4 price. Moving down the demand curve, we find at this price that the quantity demanded of tractor caps is 1,000. However, we also find that we are moving down the supply curve, and that the quantity supplied of tractor caps is 600. This clearly is not a happy situation, at least for consumers. There will be a good number of people who hoped to buy tractor caps for $4 who will be frustrated and unable find them. There will be "excess demand." This regularly occurs in countries where the market does not set prices; the same places where one sees people standing in line for goods but unable to obtain the amount they wish to purchase.

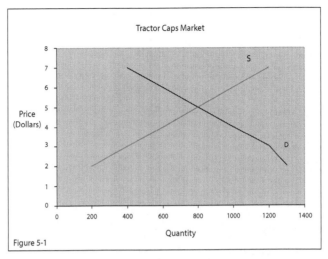

Figure 5-1

Notice that there will be a large number of people willing to buy tractor caps at a price higher than $4. We already noticed that at $5 consumers would be willing to purchase 800 tractor caps. Some of these people will offer producers more than the $4, perhaps $4.50. This will have two effects. First, the producers will see that they can get more than $4 for tractor caps. They will offer more tractor caps for sale at a higher price, thereby moving up the supply curve. Second, fewer tractor caps will be demanded as the price rises. Notice, however, that there is still an excess demand at $4.50. The same process will repeat itself for any price less than $5.

Suppose instead that the price were $6. Then we would have an excess amount of tractor caps. Producers would have offered more than people are willing to purchase at that price. In our example, producers would be offering 1,000 tractor caps, but at $6 only 600 would be demanded, and producers would have an excess supply. Most of us have lived in a market-type economy long enough to know what will happen: a "sale." Some producers will offer their product for less by cutting the price. As the price falls, the quantity demanded will increase. Of course, fewer amounts of the good will be offered for sale. We will see tractor caps marked down to $5.50, then to $5, until the number of tractor caps produced over time is the same as the amount of tractor caps that people wish to purchase. At this point the market will be in equilibrium.

It seems logical to ask if markets are ever in equilibrium. The answer can be found by looking around you. Do you see any goods or services for which there is a large excess demand or excess supply? In economies that are based on the market system, the answer is no. There may be certain times and certain products where there is excess demand or supply, but generally if you wish to purchase something at the market price, you can obtain it. When you get an instance like the 1973 gasoline lines, where people were waiting for hours to purchase gasoline, or could not purchase gasoline on certain days, it is a case where the price system has not been allowed to operate. In situations like this it is also likely that the market has not been allowed to operate because of some form of government intervention. When left to the free market, however, shortages are usually quickly eliminated through increases in price.

The same is true of excess supply of a good or service. We do not normally see unwanted inventories sitting around for lengthy periods of time. Sales, rebates, and markdowns take care of problems in the short run, and retailers then begin ordering less. Producers then have excess inventories and lower their prices to the retailer and begin producing less.

The same is true of labor services. If there is an excess of accounting services, we see salaries for accountants, especially starting accountants, going down relative to other salaries. This signals to existing accountants that they might reexamine their other opportunities, maybe becoming an attorney, a football coach, or whatever their next-best opportunity is. Students will turn to professions other than accounting, since the opportunity cost of becoming something other than an accountant has now declined.

## APPLICATIONS

HAVING LEARNED THE BASIC tools of analysis, the time has come to use them. There are three basic situations we will look at, but you will quickly notice that they encompass an infinite number of everyday circumstances. These three situations are a shift in the supply curve, a shift in the demand curve, and fixing the market price at something other than equilibrium.

Let us first observe a case of a shift in the supply curve. In August 1990, Iraq invaded Kuwait, disrupting the potential supply of oil to world markets. This led to an increase in the price of oil from $20 per barrel to more than $40 per barrel in a very short period. What do you think happened to the price and quantity of gasoline sold in the market?

Recall that a rise in the price of an input will reduce the quantity supplied at every price and cause the supply curve to shift to the left. From this shift we notice a rise in price and that the quantity sold declines. This is shown in Figure 5-2.

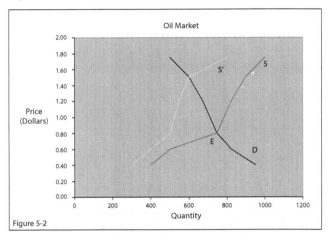

Figure 5-2

When analyzing this type of situation, we generally begin with the equilibrium conditions. In our example, then, we begin at the point labeled E, where the price is at equilibrium, and where the original demand and supply curves, D and S, intersect. The equilibrium price is $0.80 per gallon and the equilibrium quantity is 750 gallons of gasoline. The rise in the price of oil shifts the supply curve to the left, to S'. Notice that the demand curve, D, has not shifted, as we did not allow for changes in people's tastes for gasoline, changes in income, or changes in the prices of substitutes or complements for gasoline.

Look at how much gasoline would be supplied at $0.80. With the shift to S', the amount supplied would no longer be 750 gallons, but rather 500 gallons. The quantity demanded would remain at 750 gallons, however, so there would be excess demand for gasoline. As gasoline producers find that they run out of gasoline at the current price, the price will be raised and greater quantities will be supplied. Some customers will pay a higher price in order to make sure they have gasoline. Others, however, will no longer demand as much gasoline as they did at the lower price, and quantity demanded will decrease. The price and quantity supplied will continue to rise until the quantity demanded falls to the point where it is again equal to quantity supplied. This is at the price where the new supply curve, S', intersects the demand curve, D. At $1.50 the market will have again reached equilibrium, where quantity demanded equals quantity supplied, and the quantity sold in the market at this price will be 600 gallons.

For our second example of a shift in the supply curve we will begin with a question: What is the effect of an improvement in the technology of production on market price and quantity sold? When new products are introduced, isn't it usually the case that they are relatively expensive and that relatively few of them are sold? Think, for example, of television sets, videocassette recorders, camcorders, compact disc players, and other entertainment products. At first only a few of our wealthier friends have them. But we know that if we wait, the price will come down. Is there something magic about this? We now have a reasonable explanation for this phenomenon.

When these products are new, the technology of producing them is relatively primitive. As the product is developed, the technology of producing them advances, and the production methods change. This basically means that producers are now willing to supply more VCRs, for example, at each price than they would before. We represent this as a shift in the supply curve to the right.

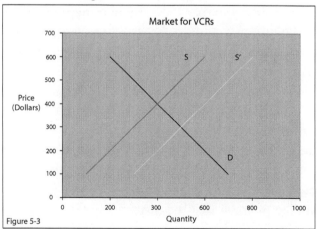

Figure 5-3

Imagine that Figure 5-3 shows the market for VCRs when they first become commercially available. The equilibrium price and quantity in the market are determined by the intersection of the demand and supply curves, D and S. The price and quantity we observe in the market will be $400 and 400 VCRs. But as the product matures (in these days at ever-faster rates) there is an improvement in the technology of production. Because of this the supply curve shifts to the right, from S to S'.

Now if the price remained at the old equilibrium price, $400, there would be an excess supply. Quantity supplied would be 600 VCRs, whereas quantity demanded would be 400 VCRs. Some suppliers would be willing to reduce their price and sell more of their product. The lowering of the price moves us down the demand curve as individuals buy more of the good and more individuals buy the good at lower prices. The new equilibrium will be at a lower price and a greater quantity sold in the market, $200 and 500 VCRs.

Let us now look at a shift in the demand curve. How can we explain the results of advertising? The purpose is to influence people's tastes for a product. A lot of advertising does not give you any information regarding the price of a product. It attempts to get you to purchase more of the product than you otherwise would have at each price. The advertiser is attempting to shift our demand so that we are willing to buy more at every given price. To the extent that advertisers are successful, our preferences will change and the market demand curve will shift to the right. This is shown in Figure 5-4.

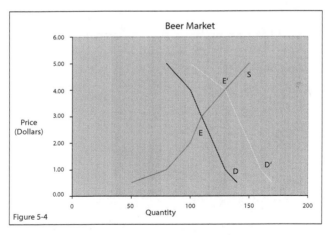

Figure 5-4

As usual, we begin with the market in equilibrium at the point E, with a price of $3 and a quantity of 110 six-packs. The advertising campaign shifts the demand curve from D to D'. By now we can see that the new equilibrium will be at a higher price and a greater quantity of beer sold.

Here the new demand curve, D', intersects the supply curve, S, at E'. The new price and quantity sold are $4 and 130 six-packs.

Let us look at another shift in the demand curve based on changes in prices of substitutes and complements. Recall that we introduced these concepts earlier in our discussion of demand. Substitute goods are those for which the demand increases when the prices of other goods rise, for example, canned peaches and applesauce. The demand for complements goes down when the price of the other good rises, for example, hot dogs and hot dog buns. Let us use this concept to show that an increase in the price of oil can result in a decrease in the price of beer, something that is not obvious to most of us.

We have already seen that oil is an input in the production of gasoline, and that an increase in the price of oil causes an increase in the price of gasoline. But gasoline is also an input into the good "pizza delivered to my house," as most pizzas are delivered by persons driving cars that run on gasoline. Thus the same reasoning we used before would lead us to predict a shift of the supply curve of home-delivered pizza to the left and an increase in the price of the good "pizza delivered to my house." Let us also suppose that pizzas are salty, and that there is nothing like an ice-cold beer to drink with my pizza. When a pizza is delivered to my house, I usually drink beer with it. This indicates that beer and home-delivered pizzas are complements. When the price of home-delivered pizza goes up, I am willing to buy less beer at every price of beer because I will buy fewer home-delivered pizzas. This means that the demand curve for beer has shifted to the left,

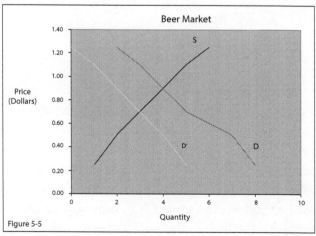

Figure 5-5

as in Figure 5-5.

The original demand curve for beer is labeled D, and the supply curve is labeled S. The shift of the demand curve is indicated by the new demand curve, D', where fewer units of beer are purchased at every price. The original equilibrium price for beer is $0.90 per bottle. The new equilibrium price will be $0.70 per bottle. This illustrates what we originally set out to prove: that an increase in the price of oil will cause the price of beer to decrease. (Note that the increase in oil prices has also caused the quantity of beer purchased to go down.)

One can create a myriad of examples of shifts in demand and supply curves and what the new equilibrium prices and quantities will be. The hard part is determining whether the supply curve or the demand curve has shifted—or if both have shifted—and in which direction. Usually common sense is a good guide. The important thing to remember is that a change in the price of a good never shifts either the supply curve or the demand curve for that good.

The final situation to look at is one where the market does not reach equilibrium. The primary cause of this is usually some form of government intervention in the market, notably minimum-wage legislation and rent control.

The price for labor is usually called the wage. As with any other good, we would expect the quantity demanded of labor services to increase as the wage falls. Since you can't pay me more than the value of the added product I produce, you are more likely to want to hire me at $4 per hour than you would be at $400 per hour.

We would also expect the supply curve for labor to slope upward. People must be paid the value of their opportunity cost in order to get them to work. As the wage increases, it is more likely that it will exceed the opportunity cost of a person's time, and thus it is more likely that he or she will want to supply their labor. Increases in the wage, then, result in increases in the quantity of labor supplied. This is shown by the upward-sloping supply curve in Figure 5-6.[1]

Suppose the equilibrium wage, where demand for labor equals the supply of labor, is at $3 per hour, as shown in Figure 4-6 where D is the demand for labor and S is the supply. And suppose that the government determines that the minimum wage anyone can pay is $5 per hour (We is

the equilibrium wage and Wm is the minimum wage). As we look at Figure
5-6, we can see what will happen. The quantity of labor demanded will be
less than was the case at $3 per hour, and the quantity of labor supplied will
be greater than at $3 per hour. This results in unemployment. The number
of persons looking for jobs minus the number of workers producers actually want (Nl minus Nd) is the amount of unemployment that will result.
The effect of the minimum wage is to cause unemployment.

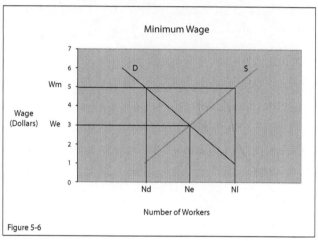

Figure 5-6

Notice also that there are fewer jobs being provided. In equilibrium
the amount of labor being used was Ne. If we assume that the government
cannot force employers to hire people, then the amount of labor being used
at $5 per hour is Nd. The people from Ne to Nd are laid off.

Next, let us look at the case where the government will not allow me
to rent my apartment at more than $400 per month. Further suppose that
the equilibrium price for rental housing is $500 per month, as shown in
Figure 5-7, where D is the demand for rental housing and S is the supply
of rental housing. At $400 per month the quantity supplied of rental hous-
ing will be Qs, and the quantity demanded of rental housing will be Qd.
Obviously, the quantity demanded is greater than the quantity supplied
(Qd minus Qs). This is called a shortage (the difference between quantity demanded and quantity supplied at the going price). In the absence of
government regulation, the market would eliminate this shortage since the
price would rise and we would move up the supply curve and down the
demand curve until we reached equilibrium. Thus rent control will produce

a shortage of rental housing.

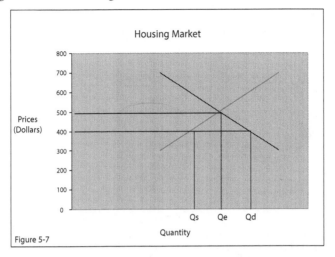

Figure 5-7

Again, the output that will exist in the market will be less than would have existed at equilibrium. The government cannot force suppliers to bring to market the amount necessary to meet the demand (unless it's a dictatorship). Whenever the government does not allow the market price to move to equilibrium there will be less output than would be the case without government intervention.

## SUMMARY

SINCE WE HAVE COVERED quite a bit of material in this chapter, a summary of some key ideas may be helpful. First, by putting the demand and supply curves together we can establish the equilibrium price and quantity that will prevail in a market. Any price lower than this will result in more of the good being demanded than will be supplied—a shortage. Any price higher than this will result in more of the good being supplied than is demanded—excess supply. In either case the incentives are to move to equilibrium.

Shifts in either the demand curve or the supply curve will create an initial state of shortage or of excess supply. The price will then change, establishing a new equilibrium price and quantity. The key to this analysis is recognizing which of the two curves, demand or supply, has shifted.

Finally, government may attempt to fix a price at something other than equilibrium. This will result in either a shortage or an excess of supply. This must also create a situation where less of the good is produced in the market than if the price had been left to move to equilibrium.

## ENDNOTES

1. One can, using a higher level of economic theory, construct examples where the supply curve will bend backward at some point. This is not important for our purposes here.

# Chapter VI

# PROFIT

THE ABILITY TO EARN profit is one of the most important aspects of a market economy. Profit not only rewards individuals for taking risks and pleasing consumers, but it also acts as a market signal in the same way prices do. Eliminate profit, and the flow of resources to their most valued use and the efficient management of resources will be damaged.

## ECONOMIC PROFIT

PROFIT IS USUALLY DEFINED as total revenue minus total cost. This is what we may call accounting profit. Economic profit, on the other hand, is the return the owner of a resource receives that is greater than the opportunity cost of that resource. In order to earn economic profit, the owner of a firm must earn at least as much from the use of the resources as he would earn using those resources in another industry. A firm, then, is making economic profit when it is earning "above normal" profit.

Suppose you own what is called a "party store" in the Midwest, a "package store" in the East, or a "liquor store" in the West. At the end of the year that accountant finds your sales were $100,000, and that the payments to all the owners of resources, such as your workers, the owner of your building, your suppliers, etc., are $80,000. She then notifies you that you earned a profit of $20,000. But at this point an economist would be unable to say that you had earned economic profit. It depends on whether or not you worked at the store and the opportunity cost of your time. If you worked at the store and could have instead made $22,000 peeling potatoes at a local restaurant, then you would have to consider this as part of your costs: you would have made a loss of $2,000.

## EFFECT ON SUPPLY

NOW LET'S THINK FOR a moment about what happens when a firm produces a product and earns economic profit. This means it is earning more from the use of its resources than those resources could earn somewhere else. Other entrepreneurs will notice that this firm is in an industry that earns more than they are earning in their industry. Some of them will choose to enter the industry where this extra profit can be made. But we already know what happens as additional firms enter the industry from our analysis of supply in chapter 3. The new firms entering will shift the supply curve for the product to the right, as in Figure 6-1.

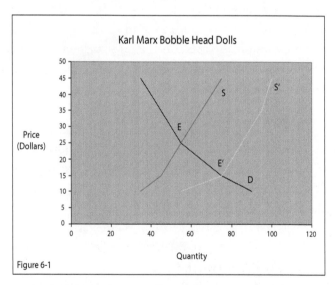

Figure 6-1

Let Figure 6-1 represent the market for Karl Marx bobble head dolls. The original equilibrium is at E, where the market price is $25 with 55 dolls per week being produced. Now suppose at this price that firms producing Karl Marx bobble head dolls are making a 12 percent rate of return on their resources, and that the normal rate of return is 8 percent. Some firms will notice this and begin producing the dolls, shifting the supply curve to the right and causing equilibrium to move to E'. At this point the price has fallen to $15, and the output is 75 dolls per week.

## PROFITS TAX

NOW, WHAT WOULD HAVE happened had we taxed away these profits? There would be no incentive for other firms to enter the industry, pushing down prices and increasing the amount of product available. As a group, consumers would be worse off because resources would continue to be used where they are less valued. But there is another problem with taxing away profits, and that is the effect on the incentive to innovate.

Notice that earning an economic profit in a market system is temporary. If a firm does not earn enough accounting profit to pay the opportunity cost of the resources used in the production of a good or service, then that firm will eventually go out of business. But we would not expect it to earn an economic profit over the long term. If it did, other firms would enter the industry, driving down prices and increasing output until all the existing firms earned no economic profit.

People and firms can earn temporary economic profits only by making above-average use of one's resources. This often means inventing a less expensive way to produce, such as improving production technology. If you are producing hats, and you invent a way of producing hats that reduces the labor cost by 20 percent, then you will be able to sell your hats at the same price as your competitors, but your costs will be lower, and thus you will earn economic profit. Eventually your competitors will find it useful to adopt your method of production, or an even better one. When they do, the supply curve for the product will shift to the right, thus driving down the price of hats and increasing the number of hats sold.

Eventually your economic profit will disappear as you are forced to lower the price of your hats to meet the challenge of your competitors. However, it will take some time for this to occur, and you will have earned economic profit in the meantime. The reward for innovation can be enormous. The lure of being able to drive a Rolls-Royce or donate millions to a favorite charity will drive people to find ways to get more output from the same amount of resources. This is conservation at its best.

Suppose you were not able to keep the profits you earned from your advancement of production technology. What incentive would you have to improve the production system? Very little—that was one of the problems with the planned economies of Eastern Europe. They ended up producing shoddy products at enormous resource costs. The environmental resources of these countries were used up at a frightening pace because there was no incentive to learn to use them better.

## THE PRODUCER'S BUDGET CONSTRAINT

WHAT IF I INVENT a better mousetrap that would have the world beating a path to my door, but I am poor and don't have financing to produce and market it? Doesn't that mean that I cannot participate in the market economy and earn a profit? No; you still have an ability to earn profit. You may not have a dime in your pocket, but if you can convince people that you have a good idea, then they may lend you money to start your business.

The market rewards risk. I will lend you money because I stand to make money by taking a risk that your idea might fail and that you can't pay me back. I may even become a partner and assume greater risk if I strongly believe in your idea.

This is where people are often confused when it comes to taxing profits. If they are taxed away there is no incentive for me to take the risk of financing your idea. By taxing away firms' profits we are not merely taking away assets from the wealthy, but also are subjecting every person in the economy to higher prices, fewer goods, and misuse of our precious resources. A tax on profit will have effects that will make us all poorer in the long run.

# Chapter VII

# THE MARKET ECONOMY VS. SOCIALISM

LUDWIG VON MISES, THE well-known Austrian economist, wrote prolifically and with great clarity about the advantages of a market economy over socialism—a system in which the state controls the allocation of resources. As early as 1922, he demonstrated that socialism could not survive as an economic system.[1] This became clear to the world with the fall of the Iron Curtain in 1989, exposing an economic system that had been unable to provide a decent standard of living for people, and that left the environment in shambles.[2]

There are three fundamental ideas from Mises. First, Mises established that a market economy allocates resources efficiently. Then, by showing that consumers ultimately determine wages, he made the point that the distribution of income is generally fair in a market economy. Finally, he showed that a market economy is the only method of organizing society to allocate resources that is consistent with individual liberty.

## EFFICIENCY OF RESOURCE USE

IN A PLANNED ECONOMY, none of this is possible. A planner can never know the vast amount of information needed to manage economic production. Just think of the difficulties that you would encounter if you were commissioned by the government to oversee the pencil industry.[3] How could you ever garner enough information to know how many pencils to make, where to produce them, where to distribute them, as well as the exact mix of resources that minimizes the cost of producing them? This might be possible if the economy were stagnant so that once you had the answers you could simply let everything roll along. But we do not normally wish our economy to be stagnant. We hope that our economy is growing. But this means that the answers to the planner's questions will change every day, perhaps every hour. As you can see, planned economies will be swamped by the problems of too much or too little information, as well as a limited capability to process it.

Nobel laureate Friedrich Hayek, in a famous paper written more than half a century ago, pointed out that knowledge exists in dispersed pieces possessed by individuals.[4] The economic problem, then, is how to make the best use of resources when people's wants, skills, and information cannot be known by any single person. An economic system cannot expect to function properly when consciously controlled by a single individual or entity; instead, the system must induce individuals to act without anyone having to tell them what to do.

There are, of course, many reason why people may not like the way the market allocates resources. For example, if you can't find a way to produce something that consumers want to buy, then you will be very poor. Those people who are unskilled, although they work very hard, may not produce anything of much value to consumers, and thus will live at a low standard of living. We may not like what the market produces with regards to disbursement of income. Like it or not, consumers may value entertainment more than culture, and thus boxers may make millions of dollars while poets make very little.

In a market economy, the distribution of income also depends on initial distributions of resources—including educational resources—as well as luck and effort. Even so, what the reasoning of Mises showed in the 1920s—and what the experience of the last twenty-five years has made abundantly clear—is that market economies will always vastly outperform planned economies. The result is that even the poorest of those in a market economy will be better off than most of those in a planned economy.

## MARKETS AS A FAIR SYSTEM OF RESOURCE ALLOCATION

OPPOSITION TO THE MARKET process often comes from two beliefs. The first is that the producers, or business owners, control the system and dictate outcomes to consumers and laborers. The second is that markets are cutthroat systems where the object is to destroy the wealth of others.

As Mises often pointed out, in a market economy, consumers are king. There is really no such thing as a production czar who can mandate how much of a good is to be produced and consumed. In a true market economy no one can force you to purchase his product, and others are free to produce any good or service to compete with anyone else's good or service.

In a market economy consumers determine the price of products and resources and the incomes of owners of resources, including labor. As Mises put it, consumers ultimately pay the wages of all individuals. A person's income ultimately depends on how well he or she satisfies consumer desires. If you are very good at satisfying consumer wants, as figures like Michael Jordan or Bill Gates have been, then you will be very wealthy. If you cannot satisfy consumer wants (suppose you are a lyrical poet who cannot seem to sell any books of poetry), then you will be poor. In a market system, those who are wealthy may not work as hard as some others, they may not be as smart, they may not be as gifted, but they certainly produce something consumers are willing to pay for.

Even those who are born into wealth must place their assets in something that produces what consumers want, if they want to keep it. History is littered with those who went from extreme wealth to modest wealth or even poverty through "bad investments." Bad investment simply means that the person's resources were put into a scheme that did not produce something consumers were willing to purchase at a price greater than the alternative value of those resources.

Nor should we believe that the market system is a fierce one of survival at the expense of one's rivals. It is not what economists call a zero-sum game, where one person wins and another must lose. In fact, markets are very cooperative systems. Just think how much you rely on others in your everyday activity. You expect that someone will grow your food, deliver your water, and produce fuel, clothing, shelter, entertainment, and the myriad of the things that you consume in your daily life. A market economy is not one of isolated entrepreneurs all attacking one another. All producers rely on other producers for inputs, delivery systems, and all other facets of the production process, as well as relying on their employees to provide the labor necessary to produce a finished product. As Adam Smith pointed out, the development of the market system allowed specialization of labor that resulted in greater output than could have been imagined under any other system. But this specialization of labor is only possible in a system based on cooperation.

## INDIVIDUAL FREEDOM AND MARKETS

THERE ARE MANY WAYS to define freedom. The Austrian school of economic analysis has as good a way as any, where individuals are free to choose between alternative modes of action. This does not mean that you have the power to choose from all possible options, but simply that you are not bound to follow the mandates of another individual.

Mises pointed out that freedom is not constrained by the laws that are necessary to maintain the structure of a cooperative society. One cannot reap the benefits of a market society and at the same time be unconstrained from actions that would destroy the market system. A law against theft does not limit my freedom because well-defined property rights are essential to market cooperation. If you are free to deprive me of the fruits of my labor or to take away the benefits from my risking my assets in a new venture, then I will have much less incentive to work or invest.

There is no real freedom other than the kind a market system provides. Economies where individuals do not own resources and cannot freely exchange goods and services, including labor services, are unlikely to be free. Resources must be allocated in an economy. If they are not allocated though free exchange, then governments will allocate them. This power to allocate resources will naturally lead to diminution of all personal freedom.

Those who would argue that government-planned economies, such as socialist economies, retain noneconomic freedoms miss the point. There is really no distinction between economic freedom and noneconomic freedom.

Consider freedom of the press. A market economy, where free exchange and access to resources occurs, guarantees a free press. On the other hand, if the government controls who receives paper, ink, and printing presses, there will be little freedom of the press. What we see today is a technological revolution that has broken down the ability of governments to control access to the resources necessary to produce information and opinion. It was this revolution, for example, that pushed along perestroika in the former Soviet Union.

As another example, what is the value of a trial by jury if the government has the ability to determine where I work? If I am charged with a crime and acquitted, the government could still send me to, say, Siberia to work at subsistence wages in a coal mine if bureaucrats did not like the verdict.

The elimination of barriers to competition preserves freedom in a market-based economy. I have a choice of whom to work for and for how much as long as there is more than one employer in the economy. In a planned economy, the government is the only employer, and thus my freedom is eliminated. I am free to choose products as long as there is more than one product and there is no barrier to entering into competition with current producers. As the late Yale Brozen, a prominent member of the Chicago school of economics pointed out, nearly all the barriers to entry are the result of government regulation and other intervention.[5]

Technology acts to reduce barriers to entry because entrepreneurs who first produce a popular product make profit. Efficient production while there is little competition creates profit. Any industry where there are enormous profits is also an industry where there are enormous incentives to enter that industry. Thus, despite, the observation of Adam Smith that "[p]eople of the same trade seldom meet together, even for merriment and diversion, but the conversation ends in a conspiracy against the public, or in some contrivance to raise prices,"[6] a market economy will naturally eliminate monopolies over time. Choice and personal freedom are natural outcomes of market allocation of resources.

## ENDNOTES

1. See Socialism, (1922; Indianapolis: Liberty Fund, 1981).
2. For a discussion of his most famous works, see Murray Rothbard. "The Essential Mises," in Ludwig von Mises, Planning for Freedom, 4th ed. (South Holland, Illinois: Libertarian Press, 1980)
3. See Leonard Read's, "I Pencil, My Family Tree as Told to Leonard Read," in The Freeman, Foundation for Economic Education, December, 1958.
4. See Friedrich Hayek, "The Use of Knowledge in Society," American Economic Review, 35, no. 4 (September 1945), pp. 519–30.
5. See Yale Bozen, Is Government the Source of Monopoly? and Other Essays (Washington, D.C.: Cato Institute, 1981).
6. Adam Smith, Wealth of Nations, ed. Edwin Cannan (London: Methuen, 1904), vol. 1, p 130..

# Chapter VIII

# A JUST POLITICAL SYSTEM

MORE THAN 140 YEARS ago, Frédéric Bastiat wrote a book titled *The Law*, in which he set forth a proposition that gives us a slightly different way of thinking about our political system.[1] Bastiat's proposition is that all government stems from an individual's natural right to self-defense. Governments are the collective organization of individuals to defend their persons, liberty, and property. He also points out that preservation of any one of these three depends on the preservation of the other two.

If governments and the laws they create and enforce are supposed to defend people and their private property, can it be just for a government to create a law that would destroy a person's right to life, liberty, and property? In particular, if law is the organization of individuals to defend themselves, can the law be used to seize an individual's property and distribute it to someone else?

Bastiat asked us to adopt a moral philosophy and establish in our own minds what government may or may not do to preserve justice. Is there really any difference between my taking your property without your consent by outright robbing you or taking your property by putting together a group in our community and passing a law that takes away your property? We need to decide how to distinguish between the two cases and the repercussions of adopting laws that enable us to take from one another.

Bastiat pointed out that there are a number of inevitable results once people allow their government to engage in the practice of taking from one person and giving to another. First, it becomes very important who makes laws. Second, it will be important to influence lawmakers who are favorable to you or unfavorable to your competitors.

We are now reaping what has been sown. In California, it costs more than $40 million to run for the U.S. Senate. How can it be that a person is willing to raise $40 million to run for a Senate job that pays less than $200,000 per year? Because the Senate seat brings with it enormous power—the power to seize and redistribute untold billions of dollars of wealth. And why should people be willing to spend thousands of dollars entertaining senators and taking them on trips to the Caribbean? Because that senator can ruin your business with the passage of a single law—or ruin your competitor's business with the passage of another law.

Corruption in government, expensive lobbying, multimillion-dollar campaigns, a Congress and state legislatures made up of lifetime politicians, and other problems of government that are obvious to most people will continue because we have accepted that it is a proper role of government (and morally justified) to take from those who are in the minority to give to those who can influence the majority of our representatives. To put it bluntly, we deserve the government we get.

To think that it is possible for Congress to pass a campaign spending law that will not favor incumbents and that cannot be circumvented by a very expensive lawyer is to whistle in the dark. The rewards from influencing government are enormous, and the larger the government's role, the larger those rewards.

Bastiat suggested in 1850, however, that it is not the legislator who is at fault, but rather the system. Scandals will continue and get larger as government's role in influencing outcomes and taking property expands, no matter who the legislators, congressmen, or bureaucrats are. Bastiat's words are just as relevant today, though written in another century and on another continent:

> As long as it is admitted that the law may be diverted from its true purpose—that it may violate property instead of protecting it—then everyone will want to participate in making the law, either to protect himself against plunder or to use it for plunder. Political questions will always be prejudicial, dominant, and all-absorbing.[2]

Today, there is a subdiscipline of economics called the theory of rent-seeking that confirms Bastiat. Economists call the practice of spending resources to influence the outcome of government in order to better one's position "rent-seeking." Many articles attempt to explain why rent-seeking occurs, estimate the loss in resources that occurs because of rent-seeking, determine the optimum method of rent-seeking, etc. But the bottom line is that as long as the government is able to create laws that subvert our rights to property rent-seeking will occur.

A second effect of accepting government's ability to take from one person and give to another is the erasing of the line between justice and injustice. When you think it is morally right for the government to pass a law that takes my property from me and gives it to you, then you must give up either your moral sense or your respect for the law. For how can you distinguish between robbery by a gang of thieves and government taking your grandmother's property through a property tax?

Bastiat labeled the situation where government power is used in violation of the maxim that government is organized to protect an individual's right to property "legalized plunder." He gives us a prescription for identifying legalized plunder: (1) see if a law takes from someone what belongs to them and gives it someone that it doesn't belong to; and (2) see if the law benefits one person at the expense of another by doing what the other person could not do without committing a crime.[3]

You might say, But shouldn't we take care of the less fortunate? What Bastiat pointed out was that being against a government taking its citizens property does not mean a person is against what a government intends to do with the property. In our example, most of us would probably say that we should help the less fortunate. But we should either do this as individuals or as voluntarily organized groups of individuals.

Politicians who wish to take the property of others to effect some outcome will often argue that if you are against the government action you are against the outcome. If you argue against the government levying taxes to provide education you are therefore against education. This is an attempt to deflect the debate away from what is the proper role of government to whether certain outcomes would be nice to have. One way of thinking about this is to ask if a politician should be able to use your money to contribute to his or her favorite charity. The answer, if one accepts Bastiat's concept of justice, is no.

Bastiat pointed out that much of what the government does is false philanthropy. It is not a true philanthropic action, whereby people freely give of their own time, talent, and treasure to assist others. In fact, the government offers a sad commentary on the condition of mankind in that it does not feel that people will assist their fellow men and women unless their property is taken by force.

Herbert Spencer, an English contemporary of Bastiat, noted that there is what might be called a lessening of our morality as a society when people rely on the government to provide assistance.[4] It is not that those receiving assistance become dependent on it, but that as individuals we begin actually to ignore those of us who are less fortunate. Rather than giving of ourselves to take care of the poor, our reaction is to say that the government takes a large fraction of our income, and therefore it is the government's responsibility to take care of them.

Bastiat broadened this concept to say that the more government undertakes and attempts to justify its expansion in our lives, the more likely it is for people to blame the government when things go wrong. People even begin to blame the government for problems the government has no power or right to solve.

The main problem with using philanthropy as a measure of what government should be engaged in is that, unlike justice, philanthropy has no limit. If you take the position that just laws are those that protect life, liberty, and property, and unjust laws are those that violate these rights, then the area of debate on whether something is the proper role of government is made considerably smaller.

If, on the other hand, government is able to do whatever is philanthropic from its point of view, then there is theoretically no limit to government's role. Under the philanthropic view, government's role is quite broad indeed.

The hard fact is that government cannot create wealth, it can only seize and redistribute it. In order to provide a grant to an artist to finish a painting it must take someone else's property. To provide education to children it must take someone's income to build the school and pay the teachers. We may decide that there are some things government can do. Yet we have to examine every government proposal and program with the view that anything government gives to one person must be taken from another.

# ENDNOTES

1. The Law (1850; reprint, Irvington-on-Hudson, NY: Foundation for Economic Education, 1981).
2. Ibid., p 18.
3. Ibid., p. 21.
4. Herbert Spencer's "The Proper Sphere of Government" was published in 1842. It is included in The Man Versus the State (Indianapolis: Liberty Fund, 1982).

# Chapter IX

# INDIVIDUAL LIBERTY

FRIEDRICH HAYEK BEGAN HIS 1960 book, *The Constitution of Liberty* by alerting us of the need to clarify our aims and principles.[1] This is even more important some fifty years later as countries in Eastern Europe, Africa, Latin America, the Middle East, and Asia struggle to establish new economic and political orders. What should these countries, as well as our own, use as a guideline to organize their social and economic orders?

The United States was founded on the guiding principle that individual liberty is to be cherished. But what do we mean by individual liberty, and why should we care about it? And if we believe that individual liberty is the foundation of a free society, how do we guarantee its survival?

## LIBERTY: WHAT IT IS AND WHAT IT ISN'T

HAYEK DEFINED LIBERTY AS the possibility of a person acting according to his or her own decisions and plans. Liberty is not necessarily having an unlimited number of options open to you. Rather, it is where a person has a set of opportunities for action with which no one can interfere.

Suppose you are very poor, grew up in poverty in rural Indiana, barely completed high school, and work at the local gas station. On the other hand, I am the son of a billionaire baseball player and have just graduated from the finest undergraduate college in the country. You may not be able to enroll at Yale Law School next year because your background and circumstances make it impossible. Yet I can choose to go to Yale to begin a brilliant law career.

In Hayek's view, we are both free as long as no one can interfere with our decisions about what to do next. Freedom lies in the fact that no one can tell you that you cannot choose to attend the local community college and work toward your goals. My freedom is similar in that no one can tell me that I cannot apply to Yale because blue-eyed persons are not allowed to become lawyers.

Wealthy people and others from privileged backgrounds may seem to have a wider range of options, but that doesn't mean they have greater freedom. You still have liberty even though you are constrained by a particular set of circumstances. This is very different from being constrained by another individual having power to veto your choice and substitute his or her will for your own.

Too often liberty or freedom is confused with power. Bastiat made the point in *The Law* that liberty is not the same as power. He used the example of education. The power to receive an education can be given by the state; but from whom does the state obtain the power to give an education? The only way the state can provide you with an education is to take resources away from other uses. And this can only be accomplished by taking money from someone else.

Hayek wrote about the confusion that people like John Dewey and John R. Commons have created when they argue that liberty is freedom from obstacles. If you define liberty as freedom from obstacles, then things quickly become confusing, and the definition comes very close to arguing that liberty is wealth. This leads to the conclusion that you can increase liberty by taking from the wealthy and distributing it among the less wealthy. But this is saying that persons should be coerced into doing things they otherwise wouldn't do— give up their property to those who wish to redistribute it.[2]

In the past, liberty had been established through the granting of certain liberties. The thirteenth-century Magna Carta, for example, limited the power of the king of England and set forth certain things that individuals could do without interference from the king. However, there is a tremendous difference between prohibiting all actions unless they are specifically allowed, and allowing all actions unless they are specifically prohibited. Life in the United States is based on the latter concept. That is, you are free to act unless a law specifically prohibits your action.

This idea is nothing new. Consider the classical Greeks. According to

Hayek, free persons in ancient Greece (not all persons were free) had five basic rights that defined their freedom. These were: (1) the legal status of a protected member of society; (2) freedom from arbitrary arrest; (3) the right to do whatever the individual desires unless specifically prohibited; (4) the right to free movement; and (5) the right to own property. This is not a bad list of rights to describe freedom in any society. Possession of such basic rights protects a person's freedom and defends against coercion.

## Why Liberty Is Important

HAVING ESTABLISHED A DEFINITION of freedom, let's be more specific about what we mean by coercion. Hayek's definition is a useful one. Coercion is when you are forced to act, not according to your own plan, but to serve the ends of another. Still the question remains, Why is it important that people be free from coercion? One obvious answer is that individual freedom is important for its own sake. But an equally important reason, the implications of which are not as immediately obvious, is that coercion eliminates the importance of the individual as a thinking and valuable person.

Hayek was very concerned about the use of knowledge in society. In an earlier chapter we discussed the wonder of the market process in that it allows production and distribution to occur without requiring vast amounts of information that encumber central planning in a socialist economy. People respond to incentives and make decisions based on prices and profit, resulting in a cooperative society that efficiently uses its resources. If there is coercion in a society, this cooperative system breaks down because bureaucrats and others in power characteristically deny an individual in the best place to make a decision the opportunity to do so. Someone less knowledgeable or less informed consequently makes the decision, resulting in a less efficient outcome. Coercion not only results in a loss of the freedom that people value, but also wastes the talent and knowledge of individuals, making society worse off than it would have been otherwise.

Lord Acton, the famous nineteenth-century English moralist and historian, is known for saying that power tends to corrupt, and absolute power corrupts absolutely. But it is not power itself that corrupts, but the power to coerce. There is a growing literature on what is meant by power but for our purposes, think of the ability of a company's chief executive to ensure that the company's product is produced in the most efficient manner. This sort of power does not lead to corruption, but rather to more products for consumers and cheaper prices.

It may also lead to more employment opportunities for laborers. A producer cannot force people to work for him. Only when government has a monopoly over employment opportunities, such as in a planned economy, is a person forced to accept a particular type of employment. This power to coerce, where you must act according to the plans of another rather than your own, is what Acton meant when he described power as a corrupting influence.

Hayek believed that the purpose of government is to provide a social order that has the minimum amount of coercion. Note there is a role for government; for a social order without government results in a life described by Thomas Hobbes as "solitary, poor, nasty, brutish, and short." Freedom is best maintained by limiting a government's coercive power to instances where it is needed to prevent other persons from coercing us. This, you may recall, is what Bastiat said; the role of government is to protect life, liberty, and property.

How is this accomplished? What sort of rules should we impose on a government that has been granted this monopoly power of coercion? Does having a democratic government guarantee a system of free people? What are the responsibilities of individuals in a free society? These are important questions that must now be answered.

## ENDNOTES

1. Friedrich Hayek, The Constitution of Liberty (Chicago: University of Chicago Press, 1960). Much of the discussion in this and the following two chapters is owed to Professor Hayek's work.
2. Of course, we have already seen that Bastiat would consider such a situation unjust since the government would be doing exactly the opposite of protecting life, liberty, and property.

# Chapter X

# CHARACTERISTICS OF A FREE SOCIETY

LIBERTY IS ACHIEVED BY setting strict conditions through which individuals grant monopoly power of coercion to their government. These "rules of the game" allow individuals to operate freely. The purpose here is not to define these rules—free people decide this—but to present guidelines for rule-making itself. In doing this we can begin to answer the questions posed at the end of the last chapter.

## CHARACTERISTICS OF THE RULES GOVERNING SOCIETY

HAYEK DEVELOPED A SET of characteristics of law that would minimize the chances of unbridled government coercion.[1] A first proposition is that rules should be known by everyone. If the rules become so complicated and numerous that the average person cannot possibly know what they are, then the people will be at the mercy of those who enforce the rules. A good example is the current federal tax code, so lengthy and open to interpretation that I cannot possibly know all the tax law, even though one of my specialties is taxation policy. Surely the vast majority of individuals who fill out their tax forms (or don't fill out them out) don't know all that is required of them under the tax code.

It is easy for a person to violate (unknowingly) one of the provisions of the tax code. For example, if you hire someone for more than $50 of work per three-month period (a babysitter for an evening once a week) then you must fill out some tax forms and withhold Social Security taxes on that person. How many people know about this, or actually do it? All of these persons could be prosecuted and face fines and/or jail sentences. The government could, if it wanted to, prosecute vast numbers of the population. By having so many laws and so complicated a legal system that we cannot know when we are in violation of these laws, we live constantly at the mercy of those who enforce the laws. As future president James Madison put it more than two centuries ago in *The Federalist Papers*:

> It will be of little avail to the people that laws are made by men of their own choice if the laws be so voluminous that they cannot be read, or so incoherent that they cannot be understood; or if they be repealed or revised before they are promulgated, or undergo such incessant changes that no man who knows what the law is today, can guess what it will be like tomorrow.[2]

Rules should also be predictable. While people should know what the law is, they should also be able to predict what the law might be in the future. The rules of the game shouldn't change frequently in ways that can't be expected. This predictability allows individuals to plan ahead.

Another characteristic of rules is that individuals should be able to comply with them. If the government were to pass a law that people could not eat, then all of the society would become a criminal. This would allow the government to pick those it chooses to prosecute and subject them to various penalties. In this way the government would have the power to coerce any individual for any reason it might choose.

Rules should also be general in nature. They should not apply to certain individuals or circumstances where it can be foreseen who will win or lose by the rules. Hayek wrote: "The law will prohibit killing another person or killing except under conditions so defined that they may occur at any time or place, but not the killing of particular persons."[3] Too often a law is passed because an individual or firm wishes to preclude some competitor from doing something, or wants to have the government transfer money to them or their cause. It is known who will win and lose when the law is passed. A free society is not one where government uses its coercive powers to pick winners and losers.

Instead, a free society requires that rules apply equally to everyone in similar circumstances. We can all relate to this basic concept of fairness. If the local politician parks his car in a no-parking zone and the parking control officer does not give him a ticket, then we are justifiably angered. We are always irritated at someone when "the law doesn't apply to them." But the reasoning behind this guideline goes beyond fairness. It ensures that those in government who determine and enforce the laws cannot use the government's coercive force on a select few.

If the rules allow government to pass laws that apply only to a minority, then it will be easier for government to be coercive. If I am not affected directly by a law, I am less likely to make an effort to oppose it. Slavery is unlikely to be enacted by law, for example, if anyone can be made a slave.

## LEGAL VS. LEGITIMATE

WHEN THESE GUIDELINES ARE followed in the rule-making process, then there will be a sphere of activity in which individuals can freely operate without the threat of coercion by individuals or government. However, being free from coercion does not mean all your actions will meet with approval. Anyone should be free to disapprove, morally, ethically, or for some other reason, with what you are doing. They are free to use the pressure of opinion in order to influence your behavior. They simply cannot threaten you with force.

This is related to the question, Should you be free to do whatever is not specifically forbidden by law, or should everything be precluded except that which is delineated by rulers? Clearly, in a society based on the first proposition, an action that is legal is not necessarily morally correct or legitimate in the eyes of society. Restricting government to using the minimum of coercion will not necessarily allow a vast amount of activity that the average citizen would not condone. Legalization does not imply legitimization. Ignoring this precept has resulted in public policy regarding a number of activities that fails to solve problems, and that unnecessarily expands the coercive power of government. The failed experiment of Prohibition in the 1920s quickly comes to mind, where government's attempt to criminalize the drinking of alcohol resulted in turning the alcoholic beverage industry over to organized crime.

Those who believe the activity is not legitimate have used the coercive power of government to prevent people from acting as they otherwise would have. Having failed in attempts to persuade people that something is immoral or harmful (or perhaps not even having attempted this route), various groups have used the power of government to force their views on others. When coercion is used rather than persuasion, freedom is reduced and a precedent for further coercion is established.

## DEMOCRACY AS A MEANS TO AN END

THE LAST CHAPTER CONCLUDED with another question: Does a democratic government ensure a free society? The answer, surprisingly, is no. Having the ability to participate in the choice of government or in the legislative process does not necessarily result in individual liberty. A "free people" is not necessarily a nation of free individuals.

Often we are led to believe that democracy is equivalent to freedom. The media has harped on the question, for example, of whether former communist countries in Eastern European are now democratic, using democratic as a synonym for free. These societies will be free when laws that are established protect individuals from coercion, whether that coercion is by an individual acting alone, or by a group using the power of government by majority rule.

The key to a free society is how to limit the power of temporary majorities. This can be done by establishing a long-term principle to which members of society agree. Hayek said that a group becomes a society not by giving itself laws, but by obeying the same rules of conduct. This is consistent with Bastiat's position that morality is necessary for a just system of laws. If there is no general consensus about a law, or at least the reasoning behind a law, then that law will be impossible to enforce.

However, democracy is also more likely to promote liberty than are other forms of government. Although the majority can still coerce the minority, there must be an opinion formed among a reasonably large percentage of the populace to allow that coercion to occur. There is nothing inherent in a majority opinion that makes it correct. You may have a profound respect for the concept of majority rule, but have strong doubts that the majority is going to be correct in its decision about a particular issue. The responsible citizens must then attempt to influence the majority. But this can only happen if there is freedom of speech. Recall Mises's point that there is no line that divides economic freedoms and other freedoms. Freedom of speech is necessary both to economic freedom and to political freedom.

## INDIVIDUAL RESPONSIBILITY

THE FINAL QUESTION WE raised at the end of the previous chapter dealt with the responsibility of the individual in a free society. Having liberty means that we must also accept the consequences of our actions. If we are free to decide what to do, then we must live with the consequences of our actions.

A free society offers choices. It does not guarantee outcomes. You have the choice of deciding whether or not to become an opera singer. If you misjudge your talent, or people's willingness to pay for your performance, then you must accept that outcome. You may starve and end up driving a taxicab. Then you may feel you have wasted all the years of training or listening to opera music. That is what freedom entails: no guarantees other than the freedom to make your own choices.

A free society demands that its people be guided by this sense of individual responsibility. When individuals are allowed to act as they see fit, people must believe that the outcomes that result from that action are the responsibility of the individual. This must be more than a legal concept. It must be similar to a moral concept, one of those general principles by which a just society organizes itself.

When people believe that individuals are responsible for their own actions, that has an effect on individual behavior. It makes people choose in a fashion that would be different if they felt they could not be held responsible. It requires them to prepare more and make more efficient choices about the use of resources. When deciding to produce a certain product and expend resources in production, they are mindful of opportunity costs. If the value is greater in other uses, then they will have paid more to produce their product than they receive for it, and they will go bankrupt. This reduces their standard of living, and they will be more careful than if the government reimbursed them for any losses they incurred.

This sense of responsibility also provides a moral justification for the manner in which society is organized. When we know that in a market system the distribution of income is actually determined by consumers, and that individuals can garner and maintain wealth only by pleasing consumers, it affects our attitude about the redistribution of income. In the same way, a sense that individuals are responsible for their actions results in a certain belief about the justice of the system.

Take that famous socialist utopia novel of the late nineteenth century, *Looking Backward 2000–1877* by Edward Bellamy.[4] Bellamy describes the economic system of late-nineteenth-century Europe as a carriage ride in which certain people randomly end up in the driver's seat, and others randomly fall off into the mud and are then engaged in pulling the carriage. It is primarily luck that determines the distribution of income in a capitalist society. If you believe this, then you probably believe it is unfair that some people are rich and others are poor and that a society should form a government that takes from the rich and gives to the poor.[5]

In a society where people are not held responsible for their actions, criminal activity, for example, is blamed on the circumstances or genetic characteristics of individuals. The belief that people who commit crimes do so by making rational choices and that they are accountable for these actions results in a much different view of criminal activity and the way society should deal with it.

Notice also that freedom is important for the altruistic individual as well as the person who seeks only personal gratification. One can hardly be considered altruistic when contributing to a cause under the threat of imprisonment. Unless you are free to choose not to contribute to a charity, and unless people believe that you are responsible for the good that occurs from your contribution, there is no room for altruism. The belief that it is a moral responsibility to volunteer one's time, treasure, and talent to the benefit of those less fortunate goes away. In a perfectly egalitarian society, there would be little altruism and a good deal of coercion.

In a free society, there is no guarantee that native ability, intelligence, or education will lead to success. In a market economy, the use to which you put your talents and resources determines what your fortune will be. If you are lazy or make incorrect choices, then you will not be as successful as a person with less talent or resources who works harder or makes better choices. This sense of insecurity is what causes people to trade liberty for guarantees. There are risks involved in my accepting responsibility for my action.

How do we ensure that a procedure of creating laws is likely to result in a free society? How do we articulate the general principle that society will follow? How can we ensure that our political system does not drift toward a coercive one? In the next chapter we will see that the advent of the written constitution provided an anchor to hold the ship of state in the bay of liberty.

## ENDNOTES

1. See Hayek, The Constitution of Liberty.
2. Federalist No. 62, in The Federalist Papers (1787, reprint New York: Bantam Books, 1982), p 317
3. Hayek, The Constitution of Liberty, p. 152.
4. Looking Backward 2000-1887 (Boston: Houghton, Mifflin and Company,1888)
5. It also presumes that people will not respond to this situation by behaving in such a way that reduces the amount of goods and services available.

# Chapter XI

# PRESERVING FREEDOM: THE CONSTITUTION

IN 1767, THE BRITISH Parliament issued a declaration that Parliament could enact any law as long as the majority of Parliament voted in favor of it. This declaration was important because it said there was no constraint upon any temporary majority that happened to control the Parliament. The concept that laws passed by a parliament would have to conform to a set of general principles embodied in a constitution had yet to be established.

Some of the American colonial leaders, such as James Otis, Samuel Adams, and Patrick Henry, objected to the declaration of Parliament because it would allow legislatures to do anything as long as a majority consented. However, Britain did not have a written constitution with which the colonists could challenge Parliament. The American colonists concluded that they needed a written document that could serve as a foundation for their colonial society.

The Constitution would serve as the document that established the basic principles under which their society would be governed. These principles would be put into action by granting certain powers to the legislative body while reserving all other powers to the people. The authors of the Constitution intended the often used and misused expression "all the power to the people" to establish the precept that the people could bind their legislative body.

## THE CONSTITUTION AS A GENERAL PRINCIPLE

ACCORDING TO HAYEK, THE American colonies were the first to put into writing the concept of a higher law directing the establishment of laws that govern everyday life. No previous society had a written document setting forth principles that would limit their legislative body's authority to create laws.

A constitution is very different from an ordinary law because it binds the legislature when making laws. The legislature should be constrained from altering the constitution. Otherwise, a constitution could be amended whenever the legislative body felt constrained, and thus the document would not serve its function. As a constitution reflects the basic beliefs of society, it should be established and amended only by the citizenry at large and only if and when that citizenry has altered its basic principles.

If the legislature does not follow any general principles when passing legislation, it will inadvertently establish such principles in an ad hoc fashion. Thus any time a situation arises similar to something that has happened in the past, it will be difficult for legislators to vote differently than they did the first time. Suppose the automobile dealers association gets a law passed that says that auto companies must buy back any unsold inventory from auto dealers. When the lobbyist for the boat dealers association shows up at the legislator's fund-raiser, it will be hard for the legislator to refuse to support a bill that would require boat companies to buy back unsold inventories from their dealers. Next, in will come the lobbyists for the farm implement dealers, the book dealers, and all other dealers one can think of. The principle will have been inadvertently established that the government should set the terms of contracts between producers and their dealers.

A constitution establishes the general principles that are agreed on by the majority of the population and binds all future majorities until such time that the majority no longer agrees with one of the basic principles. This entails a division of authority between those who write and approve of the constitution and those who make laws based on the constitution.

Power is maintained not by physical force, but by the underlying agreement of the members of society. This was pointed nearly 450 years ago when Étienne de La Boétie wrote *The Discourse of Voluntary Servitude*.[1] Writting around the same time Machiavelli was writing *The Prince*, Boétie asks why people allow themselves to be ruled by dictators. A ruler can only maintain power as long as the majority of people allow him to use that power. In the short run, military force may keep someone in power, but in the long run a person or government can maintain power only by having the acceptance of those ruled. In the same fashion, a constitution documents the commonly accepted principles and limits the power of government.

Limitations placed on a temporary majority are not undemocratic. Rather, they preserve democracy by protecting the people against those who have been granted the power of coercion. Hayek called the U.S. Constitution a "constitution of liberty" because it protects the individual against arbitrary coercion by the government.

## ENDNOTES

1. Étienne de la Boétie, The Politics of Obedience: The Discourse of Voluntary Servitude (1552: reprint, New York: Free Life, 1975)

# Chapter XII

# PROGRESS

WE HAVE LOOKED AT the market system as a means of allocating resources and—in conjunction with a constitutional democracy—determining the social order. This system has a number of desirable characteristics, including an efficient use of resources, income distribution determined by consumers, individual freedom, and a higher standard of living.

In the next three chapters we will scan the history of the Western world from the Middle Ages to the present to see important aspects of periods that encouraged economic growth. In chapter 13 we will go one step further and offer lessons from history to poor countries wishing to increase their standard of living, and to wealthy countries that are endangering their own.

## OF AXES AND CAVEMEN

LET'S THINK ABOUT HOW the first axe came about.[1] Tens of thousands of years ago, a caveman is wandering about, being chased by mastodons, living on whatever he can gather from available plants, and eating what few animals he can capture, perhaps a wounded wooly mammoth or two. Then he gets the idea that rather than using his hands or a randomly gathered rock to dig up the berries or finish off the wooly mammoth and skin it, a tool would be useful—an axe. However, making the axe, perhaps first a prototype and then a working axe, will have an opportunity cost. The opportunity cost here is time. In order to build the axe, our caveman must spend time that he could otherwise have spent grubbing for roots and finding wounded animals.

Suppose that anyone could take the axe as soon as it was finished. Then our caveman would have no axe and no food. There would be no incentive to develop and produce the axe. In order for the axe to be invented and built, there must be some system of property rights. The caveman must know that in giving up the time that could be spent foraging for food, he will obtain an axe that he can use to improve future food foraging. Sole property rights to the axe are vital.

Once property rights to tools have been established, our caveman may decide that he is better at making axes than at killing mastodons. He then builds axes for other cave people and swaps them for mastodon meat. He may give up foraging and hunting altogether to concentrate on axe-making. This specialization of labor and peaceful exchange of goods forms a foundation for economic progress. Specialization of labor is so important for progress that Adam Smith begins his famous *An Inquiry into the Nature and Causes of the Wealth of Nations* (1776) with the statement:

> The greatest improvement in the productive powers of labor, and the greater part of the skill, dexterity, and judgment with which it is anywhere directed, or applied, seem to have been the effects of the division of labor[2]

In order for this specialization to occur, there must be not only well-defined property rights, but also an institutional mechanism for the exchange of goods and services. Obviously, there must be some agreed-upon method by which the caveman may trade his second axe for fifty pounds of mastodon meat. This mechanism for trade is most fully developed in the market system. In *The Wealth of Nations*, Smith describes how interrelated a system of trade becomes under specialization of labor. He begins with the woolen coat worn by one of the common laborers and notices how it is the product of the shepherd, the wool-comber, the dyer, the spinner, the weaver, the fuller, the dresser, etc., and how each of these persons must "join their different arts in order to complete even this homely production."[3]

## INDIVIDUALISM

A SYSTEM OF PROPERTY rights and trade must develop in order for progress to occur. But there must also be a general attitude that the individual matters and is capable of affecting the outcome of events. This attitude provides the incentive for invention and innovation, and the spark of thought that leads to progress.

For thousands of years people believed that individuals were not responsible for improving their lives; some overriding authority was. This authority could be a supernatural figure, such as an ancient Greek god, or a human being with divine powers, such as an Egyptian pharaoh. This belief that individuals have no control of their own destiny stymied human initiative and individuals, excluding mythical heroes, just went along for the ride. Even heroes were forced into situations by gods and often got out of them only through the help of other gods.

Today we are used to vast advances in technology and standards of living. My grandmother was born before the invention of the airplane. There were no cars in her hometown when she was very young. She was a mother by the time television was invented. Yet before she died, she could watch the landing of the space shuttle on a forty-inch flat-screen color television with remote control and surround sound—except for the fact that space shuttle landings were so common that they came to be rarely covered in the news. We expect that these references to modern technology will seem terribly outdated when reading this book ten years from now. Yet we need to put this in perspective. The Egyptians invented sailing ships in 3200 BC. Approximately five thousand years later, people were still using sailing ships as the major means of transporting goods. Try to imagine what the primary means of transportation will be five hundred years from now, much less five thousand years from now.

It has only been in the last few hundred years that large portions of society have lived in a world where the institutions of property rights and market transactions are dominant; where people have a belief in the importance of the individual and the ability to improve their lives; and where people are responsible for the choices they make. Before this set of beliefs, progress was slow and fitful. Today progress still lags in areas of the world where the individual is subservient to society and exists for the benefit of society as a whole.

Individuals produce and progress; societies do not. The purpose of human society is to allow individual exchange, cooperation, and protection of life, liberty, and property. Thinking that the individual can be sacrificed for the common good not only impedes economic growth; it also is dangerous. It leads to tyranny, dictatorship, and wholesale slaughter. Could the killing of millions of people during World War II and the period following it, as well as the current slaughter of thousands of persons in struggling African nations occur if everyone recognized the importance of the individual? Could any country begin a war without an appeal to that country's individuals to sacrifice themselves or their friends for the good of the society?

In his book written between the two world wars, *Liberalism in the Classical Tradition*, Mises made a vain appeal to the world to adopt the philosophy of classical liberal thought as a means of averting the coming Second World War.[4] He pointed out with great clarity that a social order based on individualism and free exchange is inconsistent with armed aggression. Such a society leads not only to economic progress, but also to world peace.

## ENDNOTES

1. This example, as well as some of the discussion of the role of individualism in this chapter, was inspired by a book by Henry Grady Waver, The Mainspring of Human Progress, 2nd edition (Irvington-on-Hudson, NY: The Foundation for Economic Education, 1953).
2. Adam Smith, An Inquiry into the Nature and Causes of the Wealth of Nations (1776; reprint, Indianapolis: Liberty Classics, 1981), vol. 1, p.13.
3. Ibid., p 22.
4. Ludwig von Mises, Liberalism in the Classical Tradition (1927; reprint, Irvington-on-Hudson, NY: Foundation for Economic Education and Cobden Press, 1985).

# Chapter XIII

# A History of Western Progress

THIS CHAPTER OFFERS AN outline of economic progress in the Western world.[1] The purpose is to encourage readers to think about general trends in economic development and to relate them to dominant social and political structures of different historical periods.

In examining the history of the Western world, we will focus on periods from feudalism to the present that have fostered innovation and capital accumulation. This overview should provide a useful guide to policy makers in both developed and developing countries, in addition to the informed reader who wants a better understanding of why he or she lives in certain economic conditions.

## FEUDALISM

THE FEUDAL PERIOD IN Europe lasted from approximately 900 AD to 1450 AD. Of course, there existed a great variety of conditions across Europe during this time. However, certain generalizations give us a flavor for the period. These are: (1) feudal society was overwhelmingly agricultural; (2) political and economic authority were generally combined in the same institution, the manor in the countryside and the guild in the towns; and (3) the terms of exchange were set by custom and law and not through negotiated prices.

Most people in feudal society were preoccupied with survival. Life was basic and hard. One worked from first light until dark attempting to raise or find food. Aside from some folks who were employed in the towns as artisans or apprentices, or those who became merchants, people lived in an agricultural setting.

The primary social ordering of the time was the manor system.[2] While this system varied throughout the Western world, essentially the manor was a self-sufficient unit based on an agricultural system, basically a farm with the lord of the manor in charge. The peasants, or serfs, lived in small villages under the protection of the lord of the manor. The village was usually located in the vicinity of the manor walls. In return for the lord's protection, the serfs were essentially bound to the soil. This system was a form of servile labor called *adscripti glebae*. There were very few people who were really free. Serfs were not, for example, able to move from one village or manor to another at will. Usually they could not even marry without obtaining their lord's permission.

The serfs' primary occupation was tilling the manor land, a major portion of which was the land of the lord, called the lord's demesne. The serfs also tilled some land for themselves. This land was often in large open fields, with each peasant holding several strips scattered throughout the field. This meant it made sense for the land to be farmed in common, the serfs working together to farm the whole plot rather than trying to plant and harvest scattered individual plots. In addition, if there was plowing to be done, it required several oxen. Since few peasants owned more than one or two oxen, the plowing was done in common. This was also true of the harvesting, with the animals grazing on the stubble.

In addition to working for the lord, the peasants owed taxes to the lord, tithes to the church, and royal taxes. Thus the peasants' standard of living was sufficient to exist, but did not allow for improvements. The lord and his knights protected the peasant, and the lord in turn was supported by the peasant labor.

There was little use of money in the manor system, as there was little need for exchange other than barter. Money was only needed for those items in which the manor was not self-sufficient. What exchange did occur was at compulsory or "just" prices and wages. There were few specialized traders. People generally traded the items that they had produced themselves. For example, the wife of a serf might make an extra shirt and trade it for some candles.

An important thing to note about the feudal system is the power the lord of the manor. He determined such things as how much land each peasant could till, how much of the produce each peasant was allowed to retain, what marriages would be allowed, where peasants could locate, etc. This power of the lord over the peasant in both the political and economic systems was a serious impediment to innovation and economic development.

While important agricultural innovations did occur during the feudal period (the introduction of the heavy-wheeled plow, the use of horses in agriculture, the introduction of iron in agricultural implements, and the use of crop rotation, for example), the rate of progress was certainly slow. The entire economic and political organization was based on custom and tradition, with little incentive for innovation.

The towns that existed were dominated by the guild system. Guilds were essentially unions of merchants and craftsmen that acted to set prices, production practices, and market shares, and to limit entry into the profession. Those who were the leaders of the guilds were able to determine whether you could live in the town and if you could engage in employment there. Like the manor lords, the guilds in the towns controlled not only the economic system, but the political system as well.

If you decided you wanted to be a craftsman and produce a new product or an old product in a new way, you had to get permission from those who were producing the old product in the old way. They were in power under the old system, and would be unlikely to want to rock the boat. The odds of you getting the chance to innovate were low. The most likely outcome would be that you had only created trouble for yourself.

There was some advancement in agriculture. There were also important inventions by medieval tinkerers, and the introduction to Europe of items discovered in other parts of the world. These included the compass, the clock, eyeglasses, soap making, gunpowder, and water mills. However, the system was not one that encouraged or drove innovation. It is not far-fetched to say that if you were living on a manor in 1110, you did not expect things to be much different in 1150, or even 1220. Imagining what the future was going to be like and taking steps to be prepared for possible changes was relatively alien.

Just to get a feel for the rapidity of change, think of one of the late night movies on television that take place in the Middle Ages. There will be knights and castles, and perhaps dragons. But how often can you tell if the year being depicted in the movie is 1230, or 1375, or 980?

Part of this is surely due to our ignorance of history. But much of it is due to the fact that not much changed in that period. If you were watching a movie about Detroit, you could certainly tell if the year was 1950 or 2010, just by the type of cars driven, clothing styles, and housing patterns. We live in a period where we expect rapid change and assume that life fifteen years from now will be significantly different from today. But if we had lived in medieval Europe, we would have assumed that things fifteen years from now would be pretty much like they are today.

Although the feudal period was one of slow growth and few incentives for innovation for the vast majority of the populace, it contained the basis for economic development; the diffusion of power across the various lords and towns, and the lack of a strong central authority to stop the rise of the merchant class and trading cities. Towns and manors were only loosely organized together. Kings of the period were not absolute monarchs. They relied upon the lords for support. There was no equivalent of the Roman emperor who could command absolute power over vast tracts of land. As a consequence, Europe arrived at this new epoch of trade and expansion of world markets without a strong central authority to constrain the ability of the merchant class to seek out profits and develop their businesses.

During the feudal period, trading cities began to develop, particularly in Italy, which operated outside the feudal system of lord-ruled manors and guild-dominated towns. By the year 1200 there were several city-states in northern Italy. This development of markets began in cities because an urban population cannot be as self-sufficient as a manorial system. The existence of trading centers and the expansion of the urban population began to put pressure on the old feudal way of life.

The feudal system reached its zenith around 1300, and remained a significant but declining factor for the next 150 years. The payment of money-wages to laborers and rent to landlords began to replace the servile labor system. As early as 1035, Milan shook itself from the feudal system. The rest of Italy, the Low Countries, the Rhineland, and northern France began to witness the development of these urban trade centers. By 1367 German cities and cities dominated by German merchants formed an organization of cities called the Hansa to protect trade routes and ensure freedom of trade.

The feudal system was in part a military one and changes in military tactics helped make feudalism obsolete. Knights on horseback had been the primary weapon, and the king relied on the support of the lords and knights to wage his battles. The king in turn paid loyal lords and knights for their service primarily through the granted use of the land. For the most part this was a barter arrangement. But the trading centers, especially in Italy, began instead to use professional armies to protect commerce. This sped up the use of money exchange and the introduction of money agriculture, where the peasants were paid for their produce with money. Professional armies were also more likely to compete against one another in the development of new weapons. Some of these weapons, such as siege cannons and crossbows, reduced the advantages of a military system based on castles and knights in armor.

With the decline of the barter economy and the rise of trade, money agriculture became more and more the modus operandi. Serfs were in turn paid for their labor, rather than simply retaining a portion of the crops. As this system developed, serfs began to purchase their way out of feudal obligations and to hold land.

The fourteenth century was unusually rough and marked the end of the feudal system. There was a great famine in the early part of the century. In 1348 an epidemic of bubonic plague hit Europe, and new outbursts occurred every fifteen to twenty years throughout the century. The population of Europe declined about a third under these pressures. Serfs began to revolt, with uprisings occurring in Flanders in 1315, France in 1358, and England in 1381. Landlords competed with one another for the declining labor force. Serfs' firm ties to the land dissolved in the aftermath of severe labor shortages, created by the famines, plagues, and civil unrest.

By the beginning of the fifteenth century the feudal system in Western Europe had given way to a system of money agriculture, peasant landowners, and trading cities. A merchant class arose outside the feudal system, free to trade at negotiated prices and to assume the risks and rewards of local and regional markets.

The key to this economic development rising from the feudal system was the diffusion of power among the manors and towns. As the feudal system began to collapse, there was no central authority capable of enforcing the status quo, or limiting trade. The next period saw further development of trade and the enlargement of the class of individuals who were to determine their own destiny.

## COMPARATIVE ADVANTAGE

SPECIALIZATION OF LABOR RESULTS in greater output, and specialization of labor can only occur if people can trade. But what should we specialize in? Our intuition tells us that if I am better than you at painting and you are better at hanging wallpaper, then we could produce more if I painted and you wallpapered than if we both were self-sufficient in our home improvement. Our gut feeling is that people should specialize in those things that they do better than other people.

But what would happen if I could both wallpaper better and paint better than you? Our intuition this time might tell us that I am better off doing both my own painting and wallpapering and leaving you to your own slow devices. This, however, is not the case, as the English economist David Ricardo called attention to at the beginning of the nineteenth century.[3] It turns out that we will always be better off specializing and trading, even if I am better than you at everything. This important point is termed the law of comparative advantage. The key to understanding this law lies in the concept of opportunity cost.

Suppose you and I have identical houses and our wives threaten to bar all televised sports until we paint our respective bedrooms and wallpaper our bathrooms. It is the weekend before the Super Bowl, so we are ready for home-improvement action. It takes me two hours to paint the bedroom, and three hours to wallpaper the bathroom. It takes you, as you are relatively uncoordinated, three hours to paint the bedroom, and four hours to wallpaper the bathroom. Since I am faster at painting and wallpapering, I might be tempted to do my own painting and wallpapering. However, being an economist, I know that we will both be better off by specializing and trading services.

Why is this so? What should I specialize in? To answer these questions we need to look at my opportunity cost (as well as your opportunity cost, since you also need to know the answer). Let's call one unit of painting completing a bedroom, and one unit of wallpapering completing a bathroom. Now we must look at the opportunity cost to me of one unit of painting. It takes me two hours to paint and three hours to wallpaper. So the two hours I spend painting could get me two-thirds of the way through a wallpaper job. Thus the opportunity cost to me of one unit of painting is two-thirds of a unit of wallpapering. Now, we can do the same thing for my opportunity cost of wallpapering. To finish a wallpapering job takes three hours, and with that three hours I could do one and one-half paint jobs. So to me, the opportunity cost of one unit of wallpapering is one and one-half units of painting.

Let us turn our attention to you. One unit of painting costs you three-fourths of a unit of wallpapering, since it takes you three hours to paint and four hours to wallpaper. One unit of wallpapering costs you one and one-third units of painting, since you could paint one and one-third bedroom units in the four hours it takes you to wallpaper.

| Opportunity Cost of Home Improvements | | |
|---|---|---|
| Person | Painting | Wallpapering |
| Me | 2/3 W | 1 1/2 P |
| You | 3/4 W | 1 1/3 P |

Table 13-1

Since the opportunity cost to me of painting is less than it is for you, and the opportunity cost of wallpapering is less for you than it is for me, I should specialize in painting and you should specialize in wallpapering. The intuitive reason is that although I am more efficient than you at both things, my efficiency advantage is greatest at painting. Because I am so good at painting, it costs me more to do something other than paint than it costs you. While I have an absolute advantage over you in both painting and wallpapering, I only have a comparative advantage over you in painting.

Notice that the opportunity cost to you of wallpapering is smaller than it is for me. Although it takes you longer to wallpaper than it does me, you give up less painting when you wallpaper than I do when I wallpaper. Your opportunity cost of a unit of wallpapering is one and one-third units of painting while mine is one and one-half units.

Let's see how this example works to make us both better off. Suppose that I follow the first route and decide to be a self-sufficient homeowner, painting my own bedroom and wallpapering my own bathroom. It would take me a total of five hours. Since I won't trade services with you, you are forced to paint and wallpaper your own home as well, taking seven hours. It takes us a total of twelve hours to get ready for the Super Bowl.

Instead, suppose we are armed with the knowledge of comparative advantage. You could wallpaper for seven hours. This is the same amount of time that you would have spent doing your home by yourself. In this time you will have completed your home and three-fourths of mine. I paint both of our houses, taking four hours, and finish the one-fourth of my wallpapering job. The wallpapering will take me three-fourths of an hour. As it takes me three hours to wallpaper one full bathroom, it will take me three-fourths of an hour to do one-fourth of the job. By working together we have saved fifteen minutes of labor, since you work a total of seven hours and I work a total of four and three-quarter hours. While fifteen minutes may not sound like it was worth all the bargaining necessary to make our deal, when the principle is applied to millions of workers doing millions of different jobs, the savings are enormous.

"But wait a minute!" you might say after thinking about this for a minute. "Why did you get all the benefit of this?" Only because I have made you a poor bargainer in setting the terms under which we traded labor. In practice, the traders will determine at what rate they are willing to trade in order to share the extra fifteen minutes. You might work a little less than seven hours and I work a little more than four and three-quarter hours. The point, however, is that there is a benefit to be shared between us from trading, even though I have an absolute advantage over you in both painting and wallpapering. It will always be the case that each party will have a comparative advantage in something because its opportunity costs cannot exceed the opportunity cost of the other party for everything.

Ricardo developed the concept of comparative advantage to demonstrate that countries are always better off under free trade. If you think about it from a commonsense point of view, even if one of our trading partners puts up barriers to trade, so trade is not "fair," we are better off not retaliating. By limiting the number of trades through barriers, we are only reducing our own opportunities to gain.

## THE EXPANSION OF TRADE: 1450–1750

THE FEUDAL PERIOD DID not end on December 31, 1449. There was a gradual development of the market system and decline of the manor system. Also, these changes did not occur evenly throughout Europe (or the world). The part of Europe that Russia occupies today remained a feudal system for hundreds of years after feudalism had disappeared in Hansa cities. The periods have been chosen to make a point regarding what was generally the case in the Western world at different times.

The period from 1450 to 1750 saw a great expansion in commerce. While trading cities and substantial commerce existed during the Middle Ages, particularly toward the end of the feudal era, if one were to pick the most important economic feature of the three hundred years from the middle of the fifteenth century to the middle of the eighteenth century, it would be the expansion of trade.

Agriculture remained relatively stagnant, as did industrial production. Again, there were some advances. The invention of a simple stocking frame for knitwear increased by ten times the number of stitches that could be made. One of the greatest inventions of all time, printing with movable type, occurred in the fifteenth century. There were advancements in firearms and artillery, clock-making, and navigational instruments. But these were exceptions; invention was still relatively new.

The most significant advancements occurred where the economy was market-oriented. Even rudimentary industry was more market-based than agriculture, which was still aimed at self-sufficiency, with a few notable exceptions such as the Low Countries. The ability of entrepreneurs to benefit directly from inventions was a primary reason for the advancement that did occur. However, since a local authority could regulate industry, it did not provide individuals the freedom that existed within trade and commerce. In 1551 the English Parliament passed a law that precluded the use of gig-mils, a device that allowed increased production in the cloth-finishing trade.[4] Laws such as this were passed to impede labor-saving devices because the authorities wrongly believed that such devices would cause unemployment, and the monopolistic guilds feared the increased competition.

In trade, however, the ability of authorities to impede entrepreneurs was more limited. First, in trade across borders one authority could not impose regulations on another. Second, authorities were unable to enforce those regulations they could impose. For example, Portugal did not have nearly enough ships to preclude smuggling of goods in violation of its attempts to monopolize the spice trade. Governments simply did not possess the wherewithal to monitor interstate commerce sufficiently to effectively impede its growth. It is not surprising that trade became the engine of economic growth.

With the collapse of the feudal system, at least in Western Europe, there opened a power vacuum in that there was no strong central authority to control the rise of the merchant class and the expansion and development of the market system. It is true that King Charles I of Spain became Holy Roman Emperor (as Charles V) in 1519. However, the Holy Roman Empire really was organized into hundreds of relatively independent principalities. In addition, Charles spent a good deal of his time fighting wars to unite the Christian world and not as much time dealing with the economic system. In the end, he abdicated the Spanish throne in 1556 without having completed his task of trying to unite the empire. During this period, the economic policies he did employ destroyed the formidable Spanish Empire. The war efforts were supported by confiscatory taxation. Trade was impeded by tariffs that also were used to raise revenue for the war efforts. Thus the empire lost power and authority during this period and eventually slid into total dissolution.

The growth of specialized traders in the Western world could only have occurred with the disappearance of the feudal restrictions on movement, wages, and prices, and the expansion of markets. Indeed, those countries that had the fewest trade restrictions were the ones that developed most quickly. In the feudal period, it was the Italian city-states that had the greatest economic development as they escaped the feudal system of resource organization and were the first market economies. During 1450–1750 two small countries, England and the Netherlands, became powerful due to their willingness to give free rein to entrepreneurs. The Dutch specialized in international commerce and therefore its government could not afford to restrict the ability of the merchant class to develop markets. The cities that made up the Netherlands followed free trade policies. By the middle of the seventeenth century the Dutch shipping fleet was three times larger than the English fleet and larger than all others combined.[5] This concept of freedom from government regulation was also true of their industrial and agricultural sectors, and the Dutch became leaders in these areas as well.

England eventually became a great power as it followed a policy of political economy that allowed individuals to develop trade and innovations.

Parliament realistically lacked the power to control its domestic economy. As a result, "British entrepreneurs enjoyed a degree of freedom and opportunity that was virtually unique in the world."[6]

Many people saw the potential for personal gain and the improvement of trade through the real-life application of comparative advantage. This served as a powerful force for the development of markets. The Western world was in a state where the merchant class was able to take advantage of these potential gains from trade and did so. Those countries that had a political system that either explicitly allowed entrepreneurs to innovate and engage in trade, or were unable to enforce what regulations they did impose, developed into world powers.

Population attitudes are important in economic development. People must recognize the importance of individuals to society, and individuals must feel capable of making a real difference in life. The attitude of merchants and scientists during this period serves as an example.

We have already seen that industry had a steady improvement that was generally market-driven. Much of the major improvement in technology was in shipping. This should be somewhat obvious; shipping was an activity most free from interference, and therefore offering the greatest rewards for innovation.

By the late seventeenth century, the scientific method had been developed and was being used for purposes of improving life. But it was not until the eighteenth and nineteenth centuries that scientific knowledge was being used on a scale large enough to promote industrial advancement. Still the concept of individuals being able to understand their environment through science and to produce things that would improve their situation began to permeate a greater portion of society after the fifteenth century.

Contrast the twelfth-century peasant—tied to the soil and using agricultural practices based on tradition—with the Dutch merchant of 1650, outfitting ships, purchasing cargo in one part of the world and delivering it to another, and profiting or losing in the venture. The Dutch merchant eventually came to believe that the government should not be able to tell him where he can sail his ships, how much he can sell his products for, and how much he can pay for his products.

This belief in the individual and free trade became particularly strong in the British colonies. Britain had, through legislation such as the Navigation Acts, ostensibly put restrictions on colonial trade. However, until 1763 when King George III attempted to pay off the debt from the latest British wars, these taxes, tariffs, and restrictions were laxly enforced, if at all. As a consequence, the colonial merchants and shippers developed a sense of individual freedom that helped lead to the American Revolution and the formation of the United States of America with its constitution of liberty.

In Great Britain, the Scottish moral philosopher Adam Smith put forth the economic justification for the case of individual liberty in his *Wealth of Nations* at the same time that Thomas Jefferson was writing the Declaration of Independence. By the close of the eighteenth century, the stage was set for a major leap in the economic growth of the Western world, commonly known as the Industrial Revolution.

## THE INDUSTRIAL REVOLUTION: 1750-1880

FROM THE MID-EIGHTEENTH CENTURY until the last decades of the nineteenth century, the development of the factory system was the dominant feature of the social structure. Prior to this period, production was in what I like to call the "Geppetto model." Most people have seen or read *Pinocchio*. Recall that Pinocchio's father, Geppetto, was an artisan, a clock maker. He built his clocks in his house, the same place from which he retailed them. He did not go to work in a clock factory and return to his home afterward; neither were his clocks retailed at Wal-Mart.

Prior to the factory system, artisans working out of small shops or homes produced most goods. People who wanted to become artisans first became an apprentice and learned the trade. Apprentices might live with artisans, in their houses or in outbuildings. The factory system led to a fundamental change in the worker-employer relationship. Though the early factories were relatively small, the big difference was that a worker came in and did his job but lived somewhere outside the bounds of the employer.

This period was also a period of great population increase and movement of workers from the countryside into the towns and cities. Although the absolute number of agricultural workers did not decline, the growth in population in the cities surpassed that of the countryside. Part of this was due to the wages paid to workers in the cities. The job opportunities in the cities were greater than those in the countryside.

In this period capitalism began to flower. Individuals risked their assets in order to make or purchase machinery in the hope of producing enough to reward their risk. In order to produce, the new capitalists hired laborers who were paid more in line with their opportunity cost, since, unlike under the feudal system, they could not be forced to work for someone. People migrated to the cities despite what were deplorable living conditions by today's standards because they believed these conditions were better than those in the countryside. For most, the standard of living began to rise.

One often gets the impression that the advent of the Industrial Revolution and the beginning of a system of mass production characterized by the use of machinery and equipment decreased the standard of living of workers. Certainly life in the cities was unsanitary and cramped, and it is true that women and children worked long, tedious, and difficult hours along with the men. But this was still better than what life would have been like had the population increased and remained in the countryside. Women and children often worked long hours at hard labor on the farms as well, but wages were better in the cities.

It is difficult to make definitive statements about how fast capitalism raised the standard of living. One reason is that data was not as meticulously kept as it is today. Also, the Napoleonic wars disrupted economic development from 1795 to 1815. Nonetheless, it is relatively clear that the standard of living of the laboring classes increased from the beginning of the period. Certainly there were losers when the production system changed. If you were an artisan involved in the textile industry, you would have seen your livelihood endangered by competition from the new textile factories, which produced vast quantities of textiles much more cheaply than you could. You would have been forced to change your occupation, or find a particular piece of the industry in which you could specialize.

There are a number of reasons why we have been told by historians and others that capitalism reduced the standard of living of workers, at least in its formative years. A detailed rebuttal to those who have argued that the standard of living fell, as well as an explanation of why historians have argued that capitalism imposed an early burden on the laboring class, is found in a book edited by Friedrich Hayek titled *Capitalism and the Historians*.[7]

One explanation is that certain literature of the period reflected the views of those who were on the losing end of change. If we view the last forty or so years of America's economic history from the vantage point of an autoworker in Flint, Michigan, much of it would be a rather bleak story. If we view it from that of a person who writes computer software, it would be a rather bright story.

There is a simple proposition that can't be refuted: the advent of the factory system changed the entire economic system. If you think about it, Geppetto could probably obtain all the wood he needed to build clocks from nearby forests. But once Geppetto opened up Geppetto's Clockworks and began producing clocks for Sears and Kmart, he surely would need a number of things that didn't exist while Pinocchio was a mere shaver. Factories require greater amounts of raw materials and a method of transporting the raw materials to the factory. They require a system for distributing the goods once they are produced, since the production will be more than the local market can use. The factory system thus emerged simultaneously with improvements in transportation, raw materials production, wholesaling, and retailing. It also coincided with an increase in agricultural productivity, since factory workers now traded their wages for food that would have to be produced on the farms.

Notice that the dominance of a market economy creates incentives for all these things to happen. No one has to be told by some authority to establish the wholesale trade. Someone will realize that a gain can be made for Geppetto and him by taking Geppetto's product and dispersing it throughout the country. Geppetto, after all, is still a clock maker at heart. There is no reason to believe he can excel at distributing his product. In the old days, people came into the shop where Geppetto worked, and Pinocchio sold them the clock. Now Pinocchio's friend, Jiminy Cricket, has an incentive to market Geppetto's increased clock production for him. The same will be true for those who see that someone must figure out how to get the wood to Geppetto. There will be a potential benefit both to Geppetto and to the person who organizes and delivers the raw materials.

What else happened as capitalism began to develop? One certainly did not need a system that produced a tremendous amount of goods more cheaply if the target market were the rich. There just weren't very many wealthy people. One could, however, make money by lowering the production costs and increasing the supply of goods that could be used by the masses. The first area where the factory system and capitalism really took off was in the textile industry. This resulted in cheap cloth, so the average person could have more than one shirt. The cloth was washable, and sanitary conditions improved.

We can think of the Industrial Revolution as a shift to the right of the supply curve, as shown in Figure 13-1. The factory system and capitalism were the advancement in technology and the method of organizing production that reduced the cost of producing. Recall that as the supply curve shifts to the right, prices fall and output rises.

The period from 1750 to 1880 was one in which a large number of

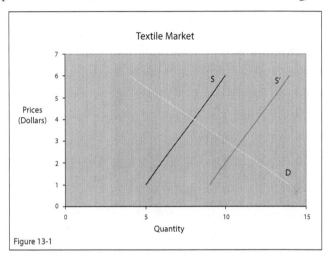

Figure 13-1

new types of goods were produced for the poor. Economic advancement in market systems has the general characteristic that goods become accessible to the poor and middle class that were not even available to the rich only a few decades ago. As Adam Smith noted at the very beginning of the Industrial Revolution:

> It may be true, perhaps, that the accommodation of an European prince does not always so much exceed that of an industrious and frugal peasant, as the accommodation of the latter exceeds that of many an African king, that absolute master of the lives and liberties of ten thousand naked savages.[8]

Think of how comfortable the average person's living conditions are today compared to those of the richest persons of the seventeenth century. The rise of the middle class was the inevitable outcome of the rise of capitalism.

## ORGANIZATIONAL DEVELOPMENT: 1880–1914

LOOKING AT OUR ECONOMIC environment, we tend to forget that only recently did industry pass agriculture in economic output. The Industrial Revolution, while a major change, did not immediately transform agricultural economies into industrial ones. The factories were small by twentieth-century standards. The need for funds to establish and expand factories could be raised either by partnerships or by the profits from the enterprise itself.

By the late nineteenth century, industrial and organizational developments favored an increase in the size of enterprises. Since there was an advantage to be gained by those who could increase the size of their operations, persons clever enough to determine how to organize their business to raise funds for replacing old factories and building new ones capable of greater output would make a profit. As is always the case where profit can be made from innovating, the innovation took place. In this era, the primary innovation was the method of organizing the firm.

During the Industrial Revolution a business entity came to be distinguished from the individual: Geppetto's clockworks came to be thought of as a separate entity from Geppetto. But it was not until the late nineteenth century that the funds necessary to put into a business became great enough to require the development of the general corporation. When there were sufficient gains to be made from the "invention" of the general corporation, this organizational innovation became inevitable.

Business organizations resembling what we might think of as corporations had been in existence for hundreds of years. The famous Dutch East India Company was established in 1602. But these were business organizations given authority by a specific writ of the government for specific purposes, often for a trade monopoly. The late-nineteenth-century corporation, on the other hand, was a business organization created to do whatever business it desired and not a privilege granted to an individual by some governmental authority.

Great Britain established some of the earliest general incorporation laws in the early 1800s, but the model for the general corporation was New

Jersey's general incorporation statute of 1891. The modern corporation allowed individuals to raise money on a scale sufficient to meet the requirement of a large production facility. One of the important elements of this business organization is marketable stock, which enables large numbers of unrelated parties to participate in business ownership.

Marketable stock allows a decentralization of business decisions. Instead of a few individuals being able to control the decision whether to undertake an operation or not, anyone can go out and sell shares of stock in the company to a large number of smaller investors. Stock provides a broader access to financial assets than would be the case if you could only get money from people you knew or from a few wealthy people.

Stock also allows individual investors to spread the risk of using their accumulated assets. I can take the money that I have earned as a clock maker and put some of it into a car company like Ford, some of it into a hot chocolate drink manufacturer like Nestlé, and some of it into a software manufacturer like Microsoft. Stock markets are the natural outgrowth of a system whereby investments are made by large numbers of individuals who stand to gain or lose by their decisions.

## THE INCREASED ROLE OF GOVERNMENT IN THE WEST: 1914–PRESENT

HISTORY SINCE 1914 HAS been one of two world wars in 1914–18 and 1939–45, and the Great Depression in the 1930s. This experience led to a decline in the belief that individualism and responsibility are the foundation for improved standard of living. As a consequence, the size of government has grown, further eroding economic progress.

As with every historical period, there is no precise date when a transition occurs, nor is the history of any era the same everywhere. But there are general trends. The United States, for example, was just beginning to levy an income tax made constitutional by the passage of the Sixteenth Amendment in 1913. The Federal Reserve Bank also started in 1913. Both these institutions are a dominant part of the American economy today. The federal debt in 1916, just prior to the First World War, stood at $1.2 billion. Even by 1970 the federal debt stood at "only" around $381 billion. Today it is above $16 trillion. At the beginning of the 1900s, spending by the United States government as a percentage of national income was around 2.5 percent. The federal government spends today about one out of every four dollars of national income. The Tax Foundation estimates that the average person works until May simply to pay their federal, state, and local direct tax burden, and this doesn't count the increased prices that consumers face due to the government regulatory burden. Estimates of the reduction in economic output due to federal government regulation exceed $700 billion. The first $500 billion federal budget did not occur until 1979. Today it is approaching $4 trillion.

There are, of course, a number of reasons for the growth of government throughout this period. Sometimes it is referred to as the growth of Leviathan, coming from a famous seventeenth-century tract by Thomas Hobbes.[9] Professor John Willson of Hillsdale College put forth an interesting hypothesis that the experience of the world wars, especially World War II, led people to become accustomed to government intrusion in the economy.[10]

This, along with the advent of Keynesian economic theory, which justifies substantial government intervention in the economy, formed the acceptance by the average person that government is the solution to the majority of society's worst social problems. Democracies reflect the underlying beliefs and general principles of people who make up a country. There should be little surprise then that recent history has witnessed a move toward large-scale government planning and control over individual lives.

## ENDNOTES

1. See Nathan Rosenberg and L. E. Birdzell, How the West Grew Rich: The Economic Transformation of the Industrial World (New York: Basic Books, 1986)
2. For a brief exposition of the manor system see Rondo Cameron, A Concise Economic History of the World (Oxford: Oxford University Press, 1989), ch 3.
3. See David Ricardo, Principles of Political Economy (1817; reprint, Amherst, NY: Prometheus, 1996).
4. For this and other examples see Cameron, A Concise Economic History of the World, ch 5.
5. See Cameron, A Concise Economic History of the World, p 114.
6. Ibid, p 159.
7. Friedrich Hayek, ed., Capitalism and the Historians (Chicago: University of Chicago Press, 1954).
8. Smith, Wealth of Nations, p 24

# Chapter XIV

# LESSONS FROM HISTORY

IF YOU WERE ASKED to advise a country that wanted to move toward a market economy and away from a socialist one, what lessons would you pass on from the last eleven hundred years of Western history? First, you could say that economic growth increased over time, its primary source was innovation, and that development of a market economy occurred over a period of centuries. Second, as the market economy spread, so did economic development. Third, in those periods where governmental authority could squash individual opportunity, there was little economic advancement, but when individuals were free to accept responsibility for their actions, there was economic advancement. Fourth, markets also provided an incentive for the development of institutions that facilitate greater economic activity. This included corporations, corporate law, financial institutions, accounting methods, insurance, the development of a system of taxation rather than servile labor, and a dependable legal system with strong property rights. Finally, there must be a separation between the economic and political spheres, so that those in political power could not restrict the expansion of markets and reduce the incentives of individuals to trade and invest.

## HARD LESSONS FOR EMERGING ECONOMIES

GOVERNMENTS THAT ATTEMPT TO move quickly from a planned economy to a market system are at a disadvantage. Chief among these disadvantages is political instability, which will threaten the government. The country's resources will have been misdirected by a planned economy; once the system is open to market forces, resources will then move to their most productive use. These resources must be released from whatever industry they were employed. In the case of labor, this means unemployment—and the longer and greater the misdirection of resources, the larger the number of folks who will be unemployed. Without a firm belief that a switch to a market economy will make things better, people will respond to large amounts of unemployment by political means, creating uncertainty and instability that will keep individuals from investing in the economy, and further exacerbating the economic problems. It is, therefore, important that the people of a country believe they can benefit from the economic changes.

Those who are in power will normally favor the status quo. If you are already in power, why would you risk losing your position by changing things? Only if you fear that if you do not change, the threat to your position will be greater or you can profit from change. Some authorities during the period of 1450–1750 began to favor the expansion of markets and trade because they found that the provision of trade monopolies and taxation was a new source of revenue to fund wars and expand their power. This aided the development of markets, since the political authority lent its favor and support. Also, much of the expansion managed to avoid the restrictions of monopoly and the burden of taxes because of the ineffectiveness of governments in policing smuggling.

Because a bias exists against change and innovation from those in power, it is necessary that the ability to innovate and produce new products be spread throughout the economy. Western economies have managed to do this through the market system. Anyone who wishes to invent a new clock has the ability to go to potential investors and try to persuade them to risk putting their money behind the development and marketing of the clock. Geppetto could go to his friends and friends of friends for support. He could go to established commercial banks, issue shares in the new company, or raise the funds in any number of ways. Geppetto does not need the approval of the Department of Commerce to produce his new clock (at least not yet).

The same has been true of Western science. Scientists can find employment in any number of ways. They may work for private firms, such as DuPont, for a nonprofit foundation, for an independent laboratory, for a university, or for any number of government agencies. The growth of Western science has been aided by this structure, namely, diffusion in the spread of ideas. If all new ideas needed the approval of a central authority, the growth of science would be slow. Look at the difference between scientific advancement during the Middle Ages, when religious and political authorities passed judgment on new ideas, and today, when markets pass judgment. The technology of toys is nearing that of the space program, as space aliens battle us in three dimensions with surround sound—all without the approval of a central authority.

## LESSONS FOR WESTERN ECONOMIES

ONE OF THE MOST important foundations for economic growth is a moral system compatible with private ownership of the means of production (capitalism) and a belief in individual responsibility (freedom). Since the beginning of the World War I, we have seen a decline in the belief that individuals are responsible for their actions and that the market system produces results that are morally justifiable. Two world wars and a depression in the 1930s provided an opportunity for those who argued the need for government planning. Such people base their arguments on a belief that individuals are powerless to improve their situations and are entitled to receive goods and services regardless of their efforts.

A lot has been written to warn us about these people. Mises, in his 1927 book, *Liberalism*, alerted us to the problems that arise from their ideas.[1] Hayek wrote *The Road to Serfdom* in 1944 about the adverse consequences of the trend toward greater government intervention in the social and economic spheres. Another Nobel Prize-winning economist, Milton Friedman, wrote *Capitalism and Freedom* in 1962 as yet another warning.[2] In the 1970s, he followed with *Free to Choose*.[3] The thesis behind these books by Friedman is simple: if authorities are able to determine for whom we may work and under what conditions, as well as what we may produce and how; if people are taught that they are not capable of directing and improving their lives, and that existing authority possesses solutions to social problems, then we will revert to the very beginning of Western economic development. As Richard Weaver pointed out in the late 1940s, ideas have consequences.[4]

The early warnings of Mises, Hayek, and Friedman may not have affected the actions of many who run the government. Yet they laid groundwork for free market advocates who followed. It may still seem that the writings of free market advocates have made precious little dent in the thinking of the average person concerning how the world works. But this is changing.[5]

Today we have numerous scholarly books and articles arguing what Bastiat was already saying one hundred and fifty years ago: government intervention in the market will lead to bigger government and an allocation of resources based on political power rather than efficiency or pleasing consumers. Rush Limbaugh, a free market advocate, now attracts more than 22 million radio listeners and his two books have been bestsellers. At the national level, free market institutions, such as the CATO Institute, the Manhattan Institute, the Institute for Humane Studies, the Heritage Foundation, the Foundation for Economic Education, and the Intercollegiate Studies Institute, have sprung up and are growing in size and number. Local and regional policy institutes, such as the Mackinac Center in Michigan and the Heartland Institute in Illinois have become influential in state and regional policy debates.

## ENDNOTES

1. See Ludwig von Mises, Liberalism in the Classical Tradition, 3rd edition (Irvington-on-Hudson, NY: Foundation for Economic Education, 1985). The first edition was published in 1927.
2. Milton Friedman, Capitalism and Freedom (Chicago: University of Chicago Press, 1962).
3. Milton and Rose Friedman, Free to Choose (New York: Harcourt Brace Jovanovich, 1979)
4. See his extraordinary book, Ideas Have Consequences (1948; reprint, Chicago: University of Chicago Press, 1984).
5. For a discussion of why this might be the case, see Friedrich Hayek, "The Intellectuals and Socialism," The University of Chicago Law Review 16, no. 3 (Spring 1949).

# Chapter XV

# THE ROLE OF GOVERNMENT AND MACROECONOMIC THEORY

WE HAVE SPENT THE last three chapters discussing progress and economic growth, but we have not yet sought precise definitions. We have perhaps understood progress and economic growth in the same way that Supreme Court justice Potter Stewart defined obscenity: "I know it when I see it."

The standard measure is the dollar value of goods and services, or gross domestic product (GDP). As an aside, think of how often you have heard one of those talking heads on network news tell you that GDP went up by some percent or other last quarter. This is usually big television news and attracts print coverage as well. Now think of how many people listening to the news, including you, could define GDP. How many of the talking heads who are telling you about the change in GDP could define it?

GDP is the dollar value of all final goods and services produced in the economy in a given time period, usually one year. Now what do we mean by a final good? A good that is either purchased by an end consumer, like a video game, or a capital good that is purchased by a producer, like a stamping mold. We only count final goods and services because we don't want to count things more than once as they move through the production process.

Suppose we produced three tons of steel in the last year and this steel was then made into two cars. At the end of the year all we have are the two cars. The steel has been used up in the production of the cars. If we were to count the steel and the cars in GDP, then it would look like the economy had produced more than it actually had.

One way to determine GDP for the U.S. economy for the last year would be to add up the value of all the final goods and services. You would count up the value of all the cars sold, all the compact disc players, all the drill presses, etc. Now you would have to be careful that if the car was sold with a compact disc player in it, you didn't count the player twice, once when it was sold to the auto company and once when the auto company sold the car. Basically you would be careful to exclude what are called intermediate goods, those goods that are transformed in the production process into other goods.

Another way to arrive at the same number is to determine what the "value added" is at each stage of production. "Value added" is what each firm adds to the value of the product as the product moves along in the production process. In simplest terms, this would be the firm's sales minus what it purchased from other firms. The standard example of determining value added is the production of bread.

Suppose a farmer begins the year with some seed left over from last year, a tractor, and some diesel fuel. The farmer sows his seed and harvests $200 worth of wheat. Since the farmer didn't purchase anything from anyone else that year, the farmer's value added would be $200. The farmer then sells the wheat to the miller. The miller grinds the wheat up into flour, then sells the flour to the bakery for $300. The miller's value added is the $300 sale to the bakery minus the $200 spent on the wheat, or $100. The bakery then takes the flour and turns it into bread. It sells the bread for $450 to the retail grocer. The bakery's value added would be $450 (its sales) minus its purchases of the flour at $300, or $150. Finally, the grocer sells the bread for $500 to its customers.

| Computation of "Value Added" | | | |
|---|---|---|---|
| Stage | Sales | Purchases | Value Added |
| Farmer | $200 | $0 | $200 |
| Miller | $300 | $200 | $100 |
| Baker | $400 | $300 | $150 |
| Grocer | $500 | $450 | $50 |
| Total | | | $500 |

Table 15-1

The grocer's value added is $500 (its sales) minus $450 (its purchases from other firms), or $50. At the end of the year, the economy will have produced $500 worth of bread—the value of the final good. If we add up the amount of value added by each producer along the way, we should also get the total value of the bread, again $500 (adding up the value added of the farmer, miller, baker and grocer we get $200+$100+$150+$50, which equals $500, the value of the bread).

Most European countries, as well as a number of other countries, use value added as the basis for their taxation of business. The United States, on the other hand, uses a corporate income tax as its primary method of taxing business activity both at the federal and state levels. Lately there has been public debate about instituting a value-added tax at the federal level. This would be a tax that each business would have to pay on its value added. As you can see from our example, the base for a value-added tax is the same as the base for a sales tax. In our example, we could either have imposed the tax on the final sale of bread or imposed the tax on the value added at each stage. In either case, the base of the tax would be $500. While we need not go into detail on the pros and cons of a value-added tax and comparing it to a corporate income tax, you will at least be one step ahead of most Americans when it comes to deciding whether your government is doing the right thing by imposing (or not imposing) a value-added tax.

Another term often used in the media and at cocktail parties, is inflation. While inflation may be like Justice Stewart's obscenity, the headline story is usually pretty specific. For example, we might read that inflation rose by 1.2 percent last month, or 3.3 percent over the last year. What do we mean then by inflation and how do we measure it?

Inflation is a decline in the value of money. This occurs when the price of all goods as a group rises. Inflation is not when the prices of some goods go up and the prices of other goods go down. This is what we have already analyzed as a change in relative prices. People often confuse relative price changes with inflation. When you can buy less of all goods with the same amount of money, then you have inflation.

Given this definition of inflation, it should be obvious that only one thing can cause inflation: an increase in the amount of money relative to goods in the economy. It is not caused by union requests for higher wages, or by increases in the price of oil, or by the existence of monopolies. All these things may change relative prices, but they cannot cause a general price increase unless they are accompanied by a rise in the amount of money in circulation. Later on we will see that in today's economies, it is the government that controls, or attempts to control, the amount of money. Thus only the government can create inflation.

There are various indices that are used to measure inflation, but the most common one is the Consumer Price Index (CPI). The media refers to the CPI when a headline tells us, "last month's inflation was 3.4% on an annual basis." Millions of people will read this headline, or hear it on the nightly news. Yet, as with GDP, few will be able to answer the question What does this mean?

The CPI is a measure of the cost of a basket of goods compared to the cost for that same basket of goods in an earlier period. The Bureau of Labor Statistics (BLS) goes out and surveys folks to find out what they generally buy. They then do a little shopping and get the prices of these goods and figure out what it costs to buy this "typical" market basket. The next month they go out and see how much it costs to buy this same market basket. By comparing the change in costs, they get a measure of inflation. If the cost went down by one-twelfth of a percent, then (forgetting about compounding) on an annual basis you have a 1 percent deflation rate. If the cost rose by one-twelfth of one percent, then on an annual basis you would have an inflation rate of 1 percent.

The CPI itself is a number that is based on a scale of 100. The BLS picks a date to do its survey of the typical market basket. The cost of the market basket is indexed to 100. One way of thinking about this is to say at that date, the cost of the market basket is 100 percent of the original market basket. If you looked at the cost of the same market basket one year later, and it was 5 percent higher, then the consumer price index would read 105, or 105 percent of the original cost. Thus, if the CPI is 286, then this means that buying the same market basket of goods today costs 286 percent of its original cost.

There are some problems with this measure of inflation. First, the typical market basket changes over time. People won't be buying the same things in 2015 that they were buying in 1955. The BLS does go out and change the market basket every few years. Statisticians then try to make the CPI consistent over the entire period.

A second problem is trying to account for improvements or changes in goods. A 1953 Ford, though an automobile, will not be the same vehicle as a 2013 Ford. A 1953 television is not quite the same product as a 2013 television. Thus part of what you are measuring in the CPI is improvement in the quality of products.

## BASIC MACROECONOMIC THEORY: THE KEYNESIAN MODEL

MACROECONOMIC THEORY IS USED to study economic aggregates, or the behavior of the economy as a whole. Items falling under the study of macroeconomics include the total amount of output produced in an economy (GDP); changes in the aggregate price level (inflation); and equilibrium conditions in the overall labor market (unemployment). Macroeconomics emphasizes the role of government in affecting these things through taxation and spending policies, and its control (or lack of control) of the money supply.

Entire textbooks are written on macroeconomics, as well as hundreds of articles in academic journals. Some economists specialize in macroeconomics and different subtopics within the field. The intent here is to provide you with enough knowledge so you can comprehend basic arguments; understand why politicians say what they say and do what they do (or don't do); make judgments about government actions; and ask a question or two of those who would argue for a given government policy.

One of my professors in graduate school, Earl Robert Rolph, used to ask a famous question of Ph.D. students presenting papers in our graduate seminar. Often these papers were done to show off a student's mathematical skill and sense of the arcane. After the student would go through some long and detailed mathematical model to reach a conclusion, Professor Rolph would ask, "Now tell me a story about why that is true."

Whenever you are presented with a complicated economic model that reaches a conclusion that doesn't appeal to you, ask the person doing the explaining to tell you a simple story about why it is true. Most models will reach results that are consistent with their assumptions. It is usually the assumptions that cause the problem.

The basic macroeconomic model owes its existence to John Maynard Keynes. He developed his theory in response to the circumstances of the Great Depression. Until the publication of his book *The General Theory of Employment, Interest and Money* (1936), the dominant belief was that the economy would reach equilibrium at full employment after any shocks push it out of its original equilibrium.[1] There could not be long periods of excess supply of labor, since wages would decline until the market cleared.

As unemployment dragged on for years during the Great Depression, the classical economists' argument for how the economy behaved lost appeal. Keynes's book posited that the economy could reach equilibrium and there still be unemployment. Keynes's explanation appeared to be more consistent with the world economy in 1936, and began to be accepted. Within thirty years Keynes's arguments, at least as interpreted by his followers, had become macroeconomic theory. Since *The General Theory* is one of those classic books that few have read but everyone is familiar with, this chapter will examine Keynesian theory from the way that it is depicted in macroeconomics textbooks.

Since the basic principle of macroeconomic theory is aggregation, you must first imagine that it makes sense to conceive that you can take numerous goods and services that exist (or might exist) in the economy and lump them all together into one good and assign a unit of measurement to it. Once you are comfortable with this basic concept, then macroeconomics begins to make sense. The basic model turns on the idea of aggregate demand and supply.

If you think of the price of this aggregated good as being the Consumer Price Index, then you are ready to think of an aggregate demand and supply curve. Using the same reasoning that we did for the demand and supply of individual products in earlier chapters, we would expect the demand curve for production as a whole to slope down. At higher prices, people will demand less and as prices fall they will demand more. Suppliers will supply fewer goods on the whole when prices are low and will supply more as prices rise. We can picture this in Figure 15-1, where AD is aggregate demand and AS is aggregate supply.[2]

Notice what happens to our aggregate supply curve, AS. At some level of output, about $400 billion in Figure 15-1, the curve becomes vertical. This expresses the hypothesis that there is some quantity of output where all the nation's resources, or at least all of its labor resources, are fully employed. No more output will be produced even if prices continue to rise. We will call this full employment output.

Equilibrium for the entire economy comes at about $350 billion in

Figure 15-1, where the quantity demanded for all goods just equals the quantity supplied for all goods, or where AD intersects AS. Again transferring the same arguments that we used in earlier chapters, at this equilibrium quantity and price there will be no incentive for producers to produce more or less or for prices to change.

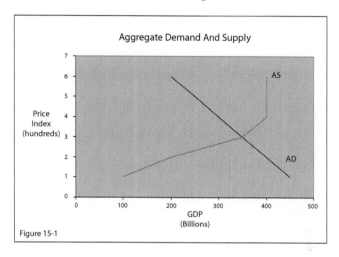

Figure 15-1

The key to all of this is that there is nothing in this model that ensures that the equilibrium level of output will be the same as the output level that corresponds to full employment. In terms of the diagram, in general, the output level where aggregate demand intersects aggregate supply will not be at the same output level as that which represents full employment. This is basically Keynes's explanation for how unemployment could have existed for several years during the Great Depression. The economy had come to its equilibrium GDP at a level of output that was not sufficient to employ everyone.

The obvious question is, How can we get the economy to come to equilibrium at an output that is equal to full employment? The answer that was most often used from roughly 1940 to 1980 was to shift the aggregate demand curve. If we can get people to demand more of the total product at every level of prices, we can get an increase in output sufficient to reach full employment. This is similar to our noting that if you advertise successfully you can get people to want to buy more of your product at every price, thus shifting demand to the right, and getting a new equilibrium at a higher level of output and a higher price. The same idea holds here.

In Figure 15-2 we see that the aggregate demand curve has shifted from AD to AD′, thus resulting in a new equilibrium where the equilibrium level of output is the same as the full employment output. Although we get an increase in the CPI, from about 275 to about 375, we get a higher level of output and eliminate the unemployment.

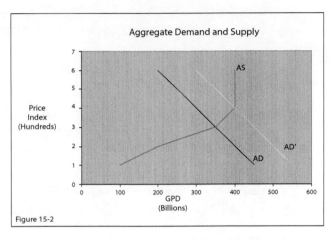

Figure 15-2

The next question: How do we shift the aggregate demand curve? To answer this question, we break down the components of aggregate demand, and then look at how we can affect each of them. In the simplest model, where we ignore exports and imports, we can think of dividing total demand for all goods into the demand for consumer goods, the demand for investment goods, and the demand for government goods. Then we can see how we can affect the demand for each of these types of goods.

Consumer goods are goods purchased for final enjoyment. These would include television sets, compact disc players, Hula Hoops, as well as services such as car repair, house painting, and lawn mowing. This would not include intermediate goods, or goods that are used to produce other goods. Now, how can we affect the demand for consumer goods?

From a public official's point of view, we could advertise, just as businesses advertise. But let us assume that businesses are already advertising at the amount that each of them feels is the correct amount. Income, therefore, is the answer. We have already noted that income affects people's demands for goods and services. The government can most directly affect people's income through taxes. That is because what people use to purchase goods and services is their income after the government has taken its taxes. Raising people's taxes reduces their spending income, generally called disposable income, while reducing taxes increases their disposable income. We would expect, then, that reducing taxes would shift the aggregate demand curve to the right, and would be one policy tool that governments can use to reduce unemployment. Of course, raising taxes will shift the aggregate demand curve to the left, reducing output and increasing unemployment, unless the economy is in the range of the aggregate supply curve where the curve is vertical.

The 1964 tax reduction proposed by President Kennedy and implemented by President Johnson after Kennedy's assassination was an attempt to move the economy out of a recession. It is often cited as a successful application of Keynesian theory in solving the problem of unemployment in the 1960s. Likewise, President Reagan's tax cuts of 1981 can be viewed as another successful application of the Keynesian model, where a substantial tax cut resulted in increased output and reduced unemployment.

Another component of aggregate demand is investment demand. This is the demand for capital goods—machinery and equipment, buildings, and inventories. These are essentially goods that are used to produce another good. There is a large body of literature on what affects the demand for goods like these. In simplest terms, the interest rate is a key determinant of investment demand. The higher the interest rate the lower the demand for investment, and the lower the interest rate the higher the demand for investment.

A simple way of explaining this is to think of what must induce you to buy a machine. First, suppose you must borrow money to buy the machine. If so, then you will have to get enough added production from the machine to pay for the cost of the loan. This includes the interest payments you must make for borrowing the money. Suppose the machine costs $100 and you borrow the $100 for ten years at 10 percent. Then the added product from the machine must generate enough money for you to pay back the $100 plus all the interest payments you make. If the interest were at 2 percent, then the machine would have to generate fewer products to make it worth your while to buy it, since the interest payments would be smaller. Thus the lower the interest rate, the better chance there is that you will find it worth your while to buy the machine.[3] Lower interest rates result in greater investment demand.

Now suppose that you are going to purchase the machine from company earnings instead of borrowing. If you had taken the money you intended to spend on the machine and put it in a bank, or bought a certificate of deposit, or shares in a mutual fund, etc., you would have earned the going market interest rate. This is your opportunity cost of buying the machine. The higher the interest rate, the greater the opportunity cost of buying the machine, and the fewer machines that will be purchased. Thus higher interest rates result in lower demand for investment goods and lower interest rates result in higher investment demand. Given that, a second way the government could move the economy out of a recession would be to lower interest rates (assume for now that it can). This would increase investment demand, which would increase aggregate demand, and thus increase equilibrium GDP.

A third component of aggregate demand is goods and services demanded by government. Examples are roads, anti-aircraft weapons, office buildings, and bridges. Government spending, which represents transfers of income from one person to another, is not part of government demand. When I pay Social Security taxes and the government gives that money to your grandmother in the form of a Social Security check, your grandmother's check ends up in her consumer demand. If we counted government spending on Social Security in aggregate demand, it would be counted twice. Only when your grandmother buys, say, a new microwave with her Social Security check is it counted as consumer demand.

When government demand increases, aggregate demand also increases, raising equilibrium GDP. (This is also the basic reasoning behind the theory that war spending by government will move an economy out of a recession or depression and toward full employment.)

We have just looked at three ways of shifting aggregate demand: (1) changing taxes; (2) changing interest rates; and (3) changing government demand. The first and third of these, taxes and government spending, are known as fiscal policy. Interest rates are changed through government changing the money supply, known as monetary policy. When you hear that government fiscal policy is loose, it means that the government is lowering taxes, increasing government spending, or both. When you hear that monetary policy is loose, it means that government is reducing interest rates through increasing the money supply (we will discuss monetary policy more in the next chapter).

## FISCAL POLICY: DOES IT WORK?

THERE IS A MOUNTAIN of literature on whether or not fiscal policy actually works. When the Kennedy-Johnson tax cut and increased federal government spending on the Vietnam War and the Great Society program was followed by the longest economic expansion in history up to that time, it appeared that Keynesian theory had won the day.

But even then, economists such as Friedrich Hayek, Henry Hazlitt, and Milton Friedman were arguing that fiscal policy was not the reason for the expansion. By the late 1970s during the Carter administration, when the country was experiencing both inflation and recession, the Keynesians were in (partial) retreat. A new school of thought that still relies on the basic Keynesian model called rational expectations came to the conclusion that both monetary and fiscal policy will not work in the long run. Milton Friedman's monetarist views, where fiscal policy doesn't work and monetary policy should only consist of stabilizing the money supply, also receive renewed attention

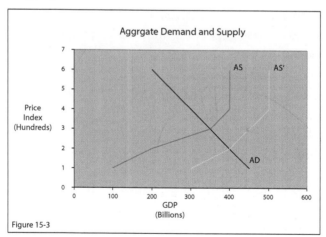

Figure 15-3

When Ronald Reagan defeated Jimmy Carter in the November 1980 presidential election, the economic policies of the Carter administration were a major factor. Some of President Reagan's key advisers were called supply-siders, because they felt that it was ineffective, if not impossible, to reach equilibrium at full employment by shifting the aggregate demand curve. They thought instead that the government should concentrate on shifting the supply curve. The Reagan tax cut was seen not as an attempt to shift aggregate demand, but as an attempt to increase the reward for producing, by reducing taxes on income, and thus shifting the supply curve out. In Figure 15-3 we can see that shifting the supply curve out will increase equilibrium GDP and lower prices.

In any event, for those who will move on to further study economics, an array of writings on the effectiveness of fiscal (and monetary) policy awaits you. Some of it is tedious, but a good deal of it is interesting.

## KEYNESIAN ECONOMICS AND THE ROLE OF GOVERNMENT

KEYNES ENVISIONED FISCAL AND monetary policy run by economists, who would increase spending and reduce taxes when the economy was at less than full employment equilibrium, and increase taxes and reduce spending when the economy was at full employment and aggregate demand was rising. Notice in this model, once you are at full-employment GDP, increases in demand just bid up prices causing inflation.

Nobel laureate James Buchanan and his colleague Richard Wagner point out one problem with the Keynesian model in their book *Democracy in Deficit: The Political Legacy of Lord Keynes.*[4] They note that in the United States, Congress controls spending and taxes, and members of Congress are elected through the democratic process. If a member promises that he will reduce your taxes and still get that road repaved in your neighborhood, then an opponent who says that if you want your road paved you will have to pay more taxes doesn't stand a chance. Thus, in a democracy, there is a natural tendency to increase spending and increase the federal debt. The Keynesian model, which says that it is the role of government to ensure full employment and that it is good policy to increase spending and decrease taxes, results in federal deficits on a regular basis.

One point to make about the role of government and Keynesian economics is that it starts with the assumption that the proper role of government is to stabilize the economy. In the basic Keynesian model, all government spending increases GDP. There is no discussion, such as we saw in Bastiat, about whether spending on agricultural research, for example, falls within the proper theory of the role of government in society. Since any government spending increases GDP, and since the role of government is to maintain the economy at full employment, nearly all government spending becomes justified.

Notice that it doesn't matter what government spends your money on. If the government hires you to dig holes and fill them up again, then government spending has increased. This increases aggregate demand and GDP. It is this feature of the model that leads to the conclusion that World War II saved us from the Great Depression. That is, hiring people to make airplanes and then fly them over to Europe to drop bombs, risking their lives, somehow made our economy better off.

When faced with such a proposition, I suggest that you follow that old professor of mine and ask the person to tell you a story about why this is true. Ask him or her to tell you a story why having people build tanks and then blow them up, or having people not produce goods for four years but instead wander through North African deserts, European fields, and Pacific jungles living in tents or sleeping on ships, killing people, and having bureaucrats ration goods, could possibly have turned the economy around. Talk to someone who was alive then about living standards during World War II. Millions of people were in military service. Consumer goods were rationed. Yet as measured, GDP was going up. But is this the way we really achieve long-term economic growth or for that matter want to live?

World War II ended the Great Depression only in the sense that it interrupted the interventionist policies of the Hoover and Roosevelt administrations, which had prolonged the economic downturn. The war placed the federal government in control of resource allocation and rationing, effectively centralizing portions of the economy. Pent-up demand for consumer goods coupled with an easing of government controls allowed the economy to truly recover from the Great Depression. Returning soldiers added to the demand for consumer goods, which heightened demand from producers for additional labor, decreasing unemployment.[5]

Keynesian economics represents a much broader view of the role of government than the Bastiat-Mises-Hayek schools of thought. A Keynesian does not even discuss whether it is the proper role of government to be engaged in taking from some people to provide others with, say, a free college education. Increased government spending on higher education, or on anything for that matter, will increase aggregate demand and thus yield a higher GDP and that is the end of it. Such a theory results in an interventionist policy that Mises says can only lead to socialism. It is why he said such nasty things about Keynes in some of his writings. It is what Hayek also warned us about in *The Road to Serfdom* and *The Constitution of Liberty*.

Most of the discussion in opposition to Keynesian policy prescriptions involves whether Keynesian policies actually work to increase GDP. But one interesting discussion topic is how Keynesian policy fits into the concept of a free society. When you are engaged in further study of the matter, or just in conversation with your neighbor, don't stop at whether policy prescriptions for taxing and spending work. Ask the question about how these prescriptions fit into our view of how a free society should be organized.

## ENDNOTES

1. John Maynard Keynes, *The General Theory of Employment, Interest and Money* (1936; reprint, Amherst, NY: Prometheus, 1997).
2. There are much more complicated ways of generating a downward sloping aggregate demand curve. The same is true of the upward sloping aggregate supply curve. These are detailed in any intermediate macroeconomics text. For our purposes, we can simply assume a downward sloping aggregate demand curve and an upward sloping aggregate supply curve.
3. Just as there is diminishing marginal utility from buying more of a good, there is diminishing marginal product from adding more machines after a certain point. When interest rates get lower, and you have to get less of a product in order to make them pay for themselves, you can add machines that have less marginal product. This is just another way of noticing that the demand for investment will go up as interest rates go down.
4. James Buchanan and Richard Wagner, *Democracy in Deficit: The Political Legacy of Lord Keynes* (New York: Academic Press, 1977).
5. For a discussion along these lines see Robert Higgs, *Depression, War and Cold War* (Oakland, CA: The Independent Institute, 2006)

# Chapter XVI

# MONEY AND THE ROLE OF GOVERNMENT

MONETARY POLICY REFERS TO government's ability to determine the money supply. In the last chapter, we mentioned that monetary policy was also one tool government can use to affect aggregate demand. As with fiscal policy, there is considerable debate about whether monetary policy is a useful government tool—and, as again with fiscal policy, little debate about the proper role of government.

## WHAT IS MONEY?

MOST MACROECONOMICS TEXTS DEFINE money as currency in the hands of the public and in checking accounts (called demand deposits by economists in order to confuse you). This is normally labeled M1. M1 is only one measure of money. There is also M2, M3, etc. M2, for example, includes M1, plus certain savings-type accounts. One can keep adding things that are further removed from what you actually use in the store to buy something.

The particular measure of money an economist might use to define money depends on what is being researched. When predicting next month's interest rates it may be that M1 is a better explanation than M2. On the other hand, it may be that guessing next quarter's GDP will require use of M2. One might use M3 to explain variations in the value of the dollar against foreign currencies. However, when you see in the newspaper that the money supply increased by 3 percent last quarter, then it usually means M1. If it says "broadly defined money supply," it usually means M2—since M3 and higher are usually used only by economists in writing technical articles.

Aside from formal definitions, we can think of what money is by using common sense: money is whatever good we use to facilitate exchange. Thinking of money this way is probably best, since doing so provides insight as to whether we need government in order to have money.

In an economy that is based on specialization and exchange there has to be a way for one person to trade their goods or services with another. If I want to buy a shirt, in a barter system I will have to find someone who has a shirt in the style I want and the size I need who is willing to trade it for an economics lecture. I know what you're thinking: who wouldn't want to trade whatever they have for an economics lecture? Even so, it would still be difficult. Money is clearly the way to get around this problem. I trade economics lectures to Hillsdale College for dollars. I then trade these dollars to the person who owns the clothing store for the shirt. This system works much better.

Money, then, is really a medium of exchange. Once we see this, other interesting points come to mind. An obvious one is that lots of different goods can serve as money. Baseball cards could serve as money if people were willing to accept them in exchange. In fact, over the centuries many different goods have served as money, even in the United States, where tobacco served as money for a period of time.[1]

Indeed, for lengthy periods of our country's history, state-chartered banks issued currency. In 1913 the Federal Reserve Act resulted in the federal monopolization of currency.

## How Do Banks Create Money?

THE FIRST PAPER MONEY was probably receipts for gold deposited with goldsmiths. Before banks, people would take their gold to a goldsmith for safekeeping. The goldsmith would issue a warehouse receipt for the gold. After a while, people would just exchange the receipts rather than the gold. Suppose you had 3 ounces of gold at Harry's Goldsmith Shop. You then buy my cottage for the 3 ounces of gold. You could go to Harry's, get the gold, give it to me, and then I could deposit it back with Harry. Or, you could just give me the receipt for the gold. In this way, the gold warehouse receipts began to be money, since they were accepted in exchange for goods.

It probably didn't take goldsmiths too long to figure out that not everybody came back to their warehouse for their gold at the same time. If they had 100 ounces of gold in their warehouse, on any given day they might have to give up 3 ounces of gold. So, why not lend out some of this gold to other folks? A merchant might come in to borrow 10 ounces of gold to purchase some silk from the Chinese, and then pay the 10 ounces back when he sold the silk to the Italians. The goldsmith could easily lend out the 10 ounces, charge 1 ounce of gold for interest and make a tidy profit. As long as all the goldsmith's customers didn't show up at the same time to get their gold, he was covered and this system worked.

This is how your bank operates today. If you put $1,000 in your favorite bank, only a fraction will stay at the bank. The bank will then lend the rest of it to someone else. This works as long as you don't have a lot of people wanting to get their money from the bank at the same time. When a lot of people come looking for their money it is called "a run on the bank." In 1933, twenty years after the Federal Reserve System began operating, runs on our nation's banks led to a financial panic.

Before we go any further, let's take a look at how the system works. Let's presume that there is only one bank, FDR Trust. This will make it easier to follow what is happening, but the result is exactly the same if there are thousands of banks. You find $100 cash in your running shorts and decide to deposit it in your checking account at FDR Trust. FDR Trust takes your $100 and opens a checking account for you for $100. The system thus begins with FDR Trust having $100 in liabilities, your checking account, and $100 in assets, the $100 cash you deposited. That would be the end of it, except for the fact that we have fractional reserve banking. Just like the goldsmith, FDR Trust needs to keep only a fraction of that $100 in reserve. It may loan out the rest, if it so wishes. The reserve requirement is set by the Federal Reserve and is changed infrequently. At the time of this writing the requirement is around 10 percent. In order to make the numbers easy to work with, let's presume the reserve requirement is 20 percent. This means that if FDR Trust has $100 in checking accounts, it must keep $20 in reserve in its vaults in case someone wants their money.

Suppose Mary comes in and wants to borrow $80. FDR Trust can charge Mary 8 percent interest and make a little money on your $100; so it loans Mary the $80. It does this by creating a checking account for Mary at FDR Trust. There is now $180 worth of checking accounts as liabilities of the bank, and the bank has $180 in assets: the $100 you put in and the $80 loan to Mary. But notice that there is now $180 in money in the economy, because checking accounts are counted as part of the money supply.

Things don't end here, however. In order to support $180 in checking accounts, FDR Trust need only keep 20 percent of $180, or $36, on reserve. This means that FDR has $64 in excess reserves. So Tom comes in and wants to borrow $64. FDR Trust creates a checking account for Tom for $64 and Tom signs the loan agreement. Now there is $180 plus $64, or $244, in checking accounts. The money supply has more than doubled since we began our story. But FDR Trust still has excess reserves. It has $244 in checking accounts, so need only keep 20 percent, or $48.80, in reserves. It may still loan out more money.

How long can this continue? If you remember anything about sums of infinite series, you will see that the final money supply can get as large as 1 divided by the reserve requirement times the original injection of money. In this case, 1 divided by 20 percent is the same as one divided by one-fifth. This is equal to 5. Multiplying the $100 you found in your running shorts by 5 results in a money supply of $500. Thus your original $100 has been transformed into $500 of checking accounts.

There are some things to notice here. First, it doesn't matter that we used one bank, since all banks are part of this fractional reserve system. If Mary had taken the $80 loan and put it in her bank, then her bank would have $80 in new reserves and $80 in new checking accounts, so it would have had $64 in excess reserves. As long as everyone's money eventually ends up in a bank, the expansion continues.

Second, the amount of the expansion depends on the bank's inclination to lend out its excess reserves. Suppose FDR Trust thought it should keep 25 percent as a reserve, even though the requirement was 20 percent. Then it would have lent out less money at each stage, and the money supply at the end would have been $400 instead of $500.

Third, the amount of expansion depends on the amount of money people return to the banking system. If you had kept $20 in cash in your piggy bank, then only $80 would have gone into bank reserves. The same would have been true if Mary had spent her loan at the hardware store but the owner of the hardware store had put $20 in his piggy bank.

Fourth, the system only works because you believe it does. If we all went to our banks and savings and loans and said, "Please give me my money," it wouldn't be there. The bank has lent your money to someone else. If you have ever seen the movie *It's a Wonderful Life*, you will remember the scene where all of Jimmy Stewart's customers come into his savings and loan and demand their money at the same time. Jimmy tells them that he cannot give them their money because it has been loaned out to provide housing for all of them. Tom's money is over in Mary's house, and Joe's money is over in Tom's house. In a dramatic scene, Jimmy Stewart persuades his customers to take only what they need out of the savings and loan, and at the end of the day he has only two dollars left in the vault. Had Jimmy not been so persuasive, the savings and loan would have closed.

In the year when this scene in *It's a Wonderful Life* takes place, 1933, there was actually a run on the banks and savings and loans. President Roosevelt shut the banks down and started federal deposit insurance. The purpose of federal deposit insurance is to keep you from asking for all of your money when your bank begins to get into trouble. The federal government guarantees that your money, up to $250,000 at this time, will be paid to you even if your bank fails. Thus you never worry that your money won't be there, and we don't all go down at once and ask for our money. Even so, if we did all ask for our money, the money would not be there. The Federal Deposit Insurance Corporation could never cover the amount of deposits that are not actually there.

## HOW DOES THE GOVERNMENT AFFECT THE MONEY SUPPLY?

THE GOVERNMENT CAN AFFECT the money supply in a number of different ways. First, it can simply create currency, Federal Reserve notes, and coins.[2] The federal government by law has made Federal Reserve notes legal tender for all debts, public and private. This means that if someone owes you $100, you must take Federal Reserve notes as payment for the debt. The federal government also does not allow any of us to create our own money; for example, my son's Wyatt dollars redeemable for 1/300 of an ounce of gold and issued by him. This means that government has a monopoly on the money supply. Since no one can create competing money, the federal government can make each of its dollars worth less if it so chooses by making as many of them as it likes. This is handy for a government if it is a big debtor, since it may pay back dollars worth less than those that it borrowed.

While publicly traded companies cannot create money, they can raise it by selling bits of ownership in the form of company stock. The private sector analogy for increasing the money supply is a stock split. Most companies split their stock when individual shares become expensive as the value of a profitable company grows over time. In a two-for-one stock split, a shareholder receives two revalued shares of stock for each share owned at the time of the split—the new shares are worth half of the old shares but the shareholder has twice as many after the split so the value of the investment in the company remains unchanged. Like the newly split shares, the value of every new dollar made by the government is taken from those dollars already in existence. Unlike a stock split, the government retains the new dollars for its own use and dollar holders see the value of the currency they hold diminish. An increase in the supply of dollars is effectively a tax on the value of every dollar in existence at the time of the increase.

The Federal Reserve has three other tools it may use to affect the money supply. It may increase or decrease the reserve requirement. When we looked at how banks create money we noticed that the amount of money created is affected by the reserve requirement—the smaller the reserve requirement, the greater the amount of money; the greater the reserve requirement, the smaller the amount of money.

Another tool is the discount rate. The Federal Reserve is a lender to banks, as the so-called lender of last resort. If a bank has not kept enough reserves and does not have enough cash on hand to give people their deposits, the bank may borrow from the Federal Reserve. The interest rate that the Federal Reserve charges its banks is called the discount rate. The greater the discount rate, the more reserves banks are going to keep. If it is very expensive to borrow from the Federal Reserve when I guess wrong about how many reserves to keep, then I will hold extra reserves. Rather than the 20 percent in our example, I might hold 25 percent, just in case one of my loans goes bad, or the timing of my loans doesn't fit the timing of withdrawals. The cheaper it is to borrow from the Federal Reserve, the more likely I am to lend out my excess reserves, as mistakes are more easily taken care of. Thus the higher the discount rate, the greater the amount of excess reserves; the smaller the money supply and the lower the discount rate, the less excess reserves, and the higher the money supply.

While the discount rate is changed fairly frequently, it often is changed as a response to market interest rates rather than a policy tool designed to influence the supply of money. If the Federal Reserve sets the discount rate at 4 percent and market interest rates move to 8 percent, then banks will be tempted to borrow from the Federal Reserve in order to profit from the difference in rates between what they can borrow at and what they can earn on the borrowings. So while it may appear that discount rate changes are used frequently to affect the money supply, they often are changed in response to market changes in interest rates.

The primary tool of the Federal Reserve is what is called open market operations. This is when the Federal Reserve buys and sells bonds. Suppose the Federal Reserve goes out into the open market and buys a $1000 government bond from Hillsdale County National Bank (HCNB). HCNB now has $1000 in additional reserves. The Federal Reserve will either give HCNB $1000 in cash to add to HCNB's reserves, or it will credit HCNB's account with the Federal Reserve. In any event, HCNB now has additional reserves since the government bond it sold to the Federal Reserve did not count as reserves. Now that HCNB has excess reserves, it will loan some out. As it loans money out it creates checking accounts somewhere in the banking system, thus increasing the money supply.

Suppose the Federal Reserve instead sold a $1000 bond to Hillsdale County National Bank. HCNB will give up $1000 in reserves in order to buy the bond, which does not count as reserves. When its reserves are reduced, HCNB can support fewer loans and thus fewer checking accounts. This reduces the money supply. Thus when the Federal Reserve sells bonds it reduces the money supply.

## WHAT HAPPENS WHEN THE GOVERNMENT CHANGES THE AMOUNT OF MONEY?

YOU MIGHT THINK THERE is unlimited demand for money, but what you're really thinking is that there is an unlimited demand for wealth or income. Money is just one good in which we store our wealth or income before we buy something. When we speak of the demand for money, economists mean the demand for money given the amount of income or wealth you possess. Your demand for money is like the demand for any other good: it depends on your income, preferences, and the price of other goods, in this case other assets like certificates of deposit or bonds. We can think of the price of money as the opportunity cost of holding it, which is what you could have earned had you bought a bond or other financial asset. This is the interest rate. And like any other good, when the price of money rises, the quantity demanded goes down, and when the price falls the quantity demanded goes up.

Just as for any other good, demand and supply determine the equilibrium price of money. If the supply of money increases, the equilibrium price of money, the interest rate, will fall as long as the demand does not shift. Thus interest rates will fall when government increases the money supply.

The standard Keynesian model has interest rates declining when the supply of money increases. Recall from chapter 14 that investment demand, one of the major components of aggregate demand, depends on the interest rate. Firms will invest—purchase machinery and buildings and add to their inventories—when the added profit from doing so exceeds the rate of interest. In this way, investment declines when interest rates rise and investment increases when interest rates fall.

Following this train of thought, the connection between monetary policy and changes in GDP is through the interest rate. If the government wants to reduce unemployment, the Federal Reserve will buy bonds. This will increase the bank reserves. Banks will increase their loans, creating more checking accounts and thereby increasing the supply of money. The increase in the supply of money reduces interest rates. Reducing interest rates increases investment demand. Increasing investment demand increases aggregate demand. The increase in aggregate demand increases equilibrium GDP, thus reducing unemployment.

By now you must be thinking, This is pretty complicated. How does the Federal Reserve know how much to increase the money supply to get to the correct equilibrium GDP? How long does it take for this process to work? What if the banks don't want to loan out these excess reserves?

Milton Friedman wrote that even if monetary policy worked in the way the Keynesian model says it works, no one can really know the answer to these questions. The Federal Reserve is just as likely, if not more likely, to make things worse rather than better. For years, Friedman recommended that the Federal Reserve just try to keep money supply growth at a constant level. There are plenty of other economists who do not subscribe to the Keynesian model. Many believe that the fiscal and monetary policy prescriptions of the Keynesian model do more harm than good and at best are ineffective because of the imprecision of the model and the inability of government to assume the responsibilities advocated by the Keynesians.

## ENDNOTES

1. One book containing a history of what has served as money is John Kenneth Galbraith's Money: Whence It Came, Where It Went (De Plaines, IL: Bantam Books, 1976).
2. Technically, federal statute requires that each Federal Reserve note be backed by collateral. This collateral is chiefly held in the form of U.S. Treasury, federal agency, and government-sponsored enterprise securities. However, this law could be changed as the debt held by the public declines.

# Chapter XVII

# THE INDIVIDUAL, THE MARKET SYSTEM, AND SOCIETY

POLITICAL ECONOMY IS REALLY a study of social order. Having moved through the chapters of this book you should now understand how society organizes its resources under a market system, a system based on cooperating individuals with specialization of labor and voluntary exchange as the foundation for interaction. The market system is not only the most efficient system of using and developing resources; it is also the only system that works in providing an increasing standard of living. The information and incentive problems of modern society cannot be solved through a planned economy. The fall of Eastern Europe's planned economies is simply confirmation of what Mises pointed out in the early part of the twentieth century.

We have learned that not only is the market system the most efficient, and in the long run, the only viable one, but it is also the only social order consistent with individual liberty. It is impossible to separate the basic freedom to choose what you will do with your time and resources from political freedom. While for some of us, individual freedom is something to be sought for its own sake, Hayek also taught us that individual liberty, and the responsibility that goes along with it, creates the most efficient use of knowledge and the most productive society.

Capitalism and the market order leads to a just society when justice is defined as Bastiat advised: there is a role for government, and this role is an extension of our natural right to self-defense. Governments that concentrate on protecting the individual from threats by other members of society and do not use coercive force to take from one member of society to give to another are "just" governments.

A market order is one in which people have the ability and the responsibility to practice true philanthropy. Our discussions of Bastiat and Hayek should make you think about what it means to be truly philanthropic. Only in a society where you own your own resources are you able to truly give of yourself and your resources. The Good Samaritan did not simply fill out his 1040 long form and rely on government to take care of the injured traveler.

The history of Western civilization demonstrates conclusively that a social order based on individual freedom and responsibility, with little coercion, led to vast improvement in the standard of living of everyone in Western society. Innovation drives economic advancement, and innovation is fostered by the market system of rewards and responsibilities. Any country wishing to improve the living conditions of its citizenry need only look to the history of capitalism for answers.

We must begin to search for answers to our problems, not in macroeconomic models of the economy, or in bigger government, but in the workings of a free society and in the writings of those who asked basic questions. As the Swiss psychologist Carl Jung once said, "Understanding does not cure evil, but it is a definite help, inasmuch as one can cope with a comprehensible darkness." Much of the problem of today's society comes about from a misplaced distrust of the individual's capacity for goodness. When we understand how individuals interact in a truly free society, we will begin to solve a number of the problems of modern society. The fall of the statist societies of Eastern Europe provides enormous opportunity for everyone, including those already living in market economies. We can learn from their failure. We must recognize where we are headed and what we are capable of as free, responsible individuals. But this can only happen when we first understand what it actually means to be a free society.

# GLOSSARY

LORD EMERICH EDWARD DALBERG-ACTON (1834-1902): Famous English Catholic, Liberal Party member of Parliament and close associate of Prime Minister William Ewart Gladstone. Most famous for writing how power corrupts leaders. Also often cited when discussing the effects of big government on liberty.

AUSTRIAN SCHOOL OF ECONOMICS: A body of economic thought originating in Austria in the late 19th century. The Austrian School developed the concepts of utility, marginal utility, and the law of diminishing marginal utility in determining the value of goods and services.

CLAUDE FRÉDÉRIC BASTIAT (1801-1850): Influential free market French economist. Bastiat developed the concept of opportunity cost and the law of unintended consequences through the "parable of the broken window." In *The Law*, he developed the concept of a just society based on economic freedom and limited government.

EDWARD BELLAMY (1850-1898): American novelist and socialist. His hugely popular book *Looking Backward* (1887) speculated on what a socialist utopia would look like in America in the year 2000.

YALE BROZEN (1917-1998): Member of the Chicago School of Economics. Business economics professor and staunch free market advocate.

JAMES M. BUCHANAN (1919): Co-founder along with Gordon Tullock of public choice theory. Buchanan was awarded the Nobel Memorial Prize in Economic Sciences in 1986.

JOHN R. COMMONS (1862–1945): Economist, labor historian, and sociologist; influential contributor in the field of Institutional Economics. Commons was a strong believer in the power of government policies to alleviate social problems.

JOHN DEWEY (1859-1952): America philosopher, progressive, psychologist, and education reformer. Dewey was major contributor to 19th and 20th century liberal thought and policies.

MILTON FRIEDMAN (1912-2006): Legendary leader of the Chicago School of Economics. Friedman was a major contributor to monetary history and economic theory, and awarded the 1976 Nobel Memorial Prize for economic science. He taught at the University of Chicago from 1946-1976.

FRIEDRICH HAYEK (1899-1992): Austrian-British economist and philosopher, best known for his classic *The Road to Serfdom*. Hayek was a prolific defender of economic and political freedom and was awarded the Nobel Memorial Prize in Economic Sciences in 1974. A member of the Austrian School of Economics, Hayek taught at the London School of Economics, University of Freiburg, and the University of Chicago.

HENRY HAZLITT (1894-1993): American economist and philosopher. His *Economics in One Lesson* is a timeless classic describing the benefits of economic freedom and limited government.

THOMAS HOBBES (1588-1679): English philosopher, who though Royalist during the English Civil War also developed many ideas that are associated with classical literature, and libertarian, thought. His book *Leviathan* is famous for its description of life without a big, strong government ("solitary, poor, nasty, brutish, and short"), but also for the idea that government is instituted to protect the individual from coercion and governs through the consent of the people.

WILLIAM STANLEY JEVONS (1835–1882): British economist who laid the foundation for marginal utility analysis along with Menger and Walras. Taught political economy at what later became Manchester University and also at University College, London.

JOHN MAYNARD KEYNES (1883-1946): Founder of Keynesian economics and one of the most influential economists of the 20th century. Keynes wrote the classic *The General Theory of Employment, Interest, and Money*. He became a member of the British House of Lords in 1942, assuming the title Baron Keynes of Tilton, which is why he is alternatively referred to as Lord Keynes.

KEYNESIAN ECONOMICS: A school of economic thought based on the theories John Maynard Keynes and his followers in Britain and America that formed the basis of macroeconomics teaching and policy from the 1930s onwards. Central to Keynesian economics is the importance of government spending and monetary policy in maintaining aggregate demand and full employment.

CARL MENGER (1840-1921): Founder of the Austrian School of Economics. Menger developed the concept of "subjective theory of value" similar to marginal utility, and is credited alongside Jevons and Walras with discovering utility theory.

ALFRED MARSHALL (1842-1924): Leading figure in the development of microeconomics. Marshall wrote that the price and output of a good was determined by both supply and demand curves intersecting like scissor blades. Marshall also developed the concept of price elasticity of demand; and consumer and producer surpluses, an early development in the branch of economics termed welfare economics. His *Principles of Economics* was the leading British textbook in economics for decades. Marshall taught at Cambridge University and was responsible for establishing economic as a separate course of study at the university.

LEGISLATION OF 1913: Pivotal year in terms of government economic policy. Congress enacted the Revenue Act of 1913, which re-introduced the federal income tax (after ratification of the Sixteenth Amendment to the Constitution in February 1913) and the Federal Reserve Act, which created the Federal Reserve System.

LUDWIG VON MISES (1881-1973): Leading member of the Austrian School of Economics. Strong advocated for free markets and limited government; predicted as early as 1922 the failure of socialism. Mises taught at the University of Vienna, the Graduate Institute of International Studies in Geneva, Switzerland, and New York University.

MONETARISM: A school of economic thought that considers money supply the principle determinant of short-term aggregate demand. For monetarists, economic stability is achieved through controlling the rate of growth of the money supply, not through fiscal policy, which Keynesians believe.

PUBLIC CHOICE THEORY: A school of economic thought that applies economic theory to politics.

RATIONAL EXPECTATIONS: Economic theory that rational economic behavior is based on expectations of future conditions and behavior.

REVENUE ACT OF 1964 (KENNEDY TAX CUT): Reduced top marginal rate from 91% to 70% and the corporate tax rate from 52% to 48%. Initially proposed in 1963 by President John F. Kennedy but signed by President Lyndon B. Johnson after President Kennedy's assassination on November 1963. The Kennedy Tax Cut is still considered one of the high water marks for Keynesian economics and government economic stimulus plans.

ECONOMIC RECOVERY TAX ACT OF 1981 (REAGAN TAX CUT): Legislation signed by President Ronald Reagan that cut marginal tax rates across the board; from 70% to 50% at the top rate and 14% to 11% at the bottom rate. The Reagan Tax Cut is considered one the key policies proving the effectiveness of Supply-Side Economics.

DAVID RICARDO (1772-1823): Influential British economist, who's theory of comparative advantage is still central to understanding the benefits of free trade.

ADAM SMITH (1723-1790): Legendary Scottish economist, who's *Wealth of Nations* in 1776, was one of the most influential books in the history of economic thought.

SUPPLY-SIDE ECONOMICS: A body of economic thought that stresses the importance of low marginal tax rates and less government spending and regulation in maintaining economic growth. Supply-Side Economics rejects the Keynesian view of government in maintaining economic growth and full employment.

LÉON WALRAS (1834–1910): French mathematical economist and founder of general equilibrium theory. Walras viewed all markets as interrelated, tending toward equilibrium through a process famously termed *tâtonnement*. Walras along with Vilfredo Pareto developed the Mathematical School of Economics also referred to as The Lausanne School. He also developed the concept of marginal utility, along with (and independent of) Jevons and Menger.

# INDEX

# M

M1  111
M2  111
M3  111
Machiavelli  69
  Prince, The  69
Mackinac Center (Michigan)  96
macroeconomics  101, 102, 110, 111,
    124
macroeconomic theory  101, 102
Madison, James  62
  Federalist Papers, The  62, 67
Magna Carta  58
Manhattan Institute, The  96
manor system  76, 83, 92
marginal analysis  11
marginal benefit  11, 12, 28
  marginal benefit curve  12
  marginal benefits  12, 13, 23
marginal cost  11, 12, 13, 28
  marginal cost curve  12, 28
  marginal costs  12, 23
Marketable stock  91
market basket  100
market demand  15, 19, 20, 22, 37
market economy  2, 8, 10, 26, 27, 43, 46,
    47, 48, 49, 50, 51, 66, 88, 93, 94
market equilibrium  14, 32
market price  20, 32, 34, 36, 41, 44
market process  7, 13, 48, 59
market supply  20, 28
market system  2, 3, 34, 45, 49, 50, 65,
    71, 72, 83, 84, 93, 94, 95, 120, 121
Marshall, Alfred  13, 124
Marx, Karl  44
  Karl Marx bobble head dolls  44
Menger, Carl  11, 23, 124
merchant class  78, 79, 84, 85
Middle Ages  71, 77, 83, 95
Mises, Ludwig von  23, 47, 51, 74, 125
  Liberalism in the Classical Tradition
    74, 96
  Mises  23, 47, 48, 49, 50, 51, 64, 74, 95,
    109, 120, 125

Monetarism  125
monetary policy  106, 107, 111, 118, 124
  changing the money supply  106
money supply  101, 106, 107, 111, 114,
    115, 116, 117, 118, 125
Monty Python  2
  The Life of Brian  2
Moses  3

# N

Napoleonic wars  87
Navigation Acts  86
  restrictions on colonial trade  86
nonhuman resources  26
normal good  16

# O

Occupy Wall Street  2
opportunity cost  24, 25, 26, 27, 34, 39,
    43, 45, 71, 80, 81, 82, 87, 106,
    117, 122
Opportunity cost  24
organizational developments  90
Otis, James  68

# P

paper money  112
Parliament  68, 83, 85
perestroika  50
personal freedom  50, 51
philanthropic view  55
philanthropy  55, 121
Pinocchio  86, 88
  Geppetto  86, 88, 90, 94
planned economy  47, 48, 51, 60, 93, 120
  government-planned economies  50
price elasticity  20, 21, 22, 124
price for labor  39
price of resources  29
price of substitutes  16
profit  8, 43, 44, 45, 46, 51, 59, 90, 94,
    113, 117, 118
  taxing profits  46
property rights  3, 50, 72, 73, 93

# W

# Z

Read on for an excerpt from Tom Grace's newest thriller

# THE LIBERTY INTRIGUE

Published by Dunlap Goddard


In *The Liberty Intrigue*, author Tom Grace serves up a fiercely entertaining political thriller. He has crafted a compelling, fast-paced, wide-ranging political thriller with gripping twists and turns, high-tech schemes, dastardly corruption, and murder. ...an intelligent articulation of the conservative philosophy.
**—Mike Brownfield,** *The Heritage Foundation*

...The latest in that line [of election novels], and certainly one of the most "outside-the-box" of political thrillers, is Tom Grace's *The Liberty Intrigue*. *The Liberty Intrigue* contains so many thrills and so much fun that one will start to say: "Hey, it's too late in '12. But can we find Ross Egan for '16?"
**—John Gizzi,** *Human Events*

*The Liberty Intrigue* is wildly entertaining and thoroughly edifying. Tom Grace spins a dazzling thriller that races across the dangerous terrain of a US presidential election with style and aplomb. A celebration of American exceptionalism found only in the power of the individual—a yarn you can't put down. Simply awesome.
**—David Limbaugh,** *NY Times #1 bestselling author*

Fresh, intelligent, and emotional, *The Liberty Intrigue* is a gem of a read. Tom Grace explores his brilliantly conceived political landscape with wit and intelligence. All of the right elements combine for an evocative tale that will leave you panting for more.
**—Steve Berry,** *NY Times #1 bestselling author*

# I

"TODAY WILL BE A good day."

Kwame Gyasi Cudjoe, the Most Exalted Excellency and Supreme Leader of the Democratic Republic of Safo, made this pronouncement from an ergonomic recliner wrapped in the leather cut from the hide of an endangered African elephant that he had personally hunted and killed. Cudjoe's flying throne was bolted to the floor in the salon of the presidential helicopter. A standard Russian-made Mi-26P helicopter could carry sixty-three passengers, but the amenities added for the comfort and protection of the African leader cut that number in half.

Cudjoe's powerful frame was clad in khaki fatigues and his combat boots gleamed like polished black onyx. No cartoon general, the strongman wore a single star on his battle dress uniform that he earned during a storied military career, one that ended with the coup d'état that won him control of the entire nation. He wore dark sunglasses, despite the shades being drawn over the porthole windows, and slowly swirled a glass of English whiskey in his left hand.

The Safolese dictator traveled light today, his only guest on the flight from the capital being a swarthy Iraqi named Latif.

"I think you will be quite satisfied with the demonstration, Excellency," Latif said, his eyes on the metal briefcase beside Cudjoe's throne.

"That is what I am paying you for," Cudjoe replied. "Satisfaction."

Officially, Latif was an engineering consultant to the Safolese government, employed for his expertise in mining and mineral extraction. One of Cudjoe's first official acts after seizing control of the country was to nationalize the mines. After all, maintaining a steady flow of gold and diamonds from the earth was essential to replenishing the nation's coffers.

Few aside from Cudjoe knew that the engineer's identity was a fabrication to conceal a fugitive. Prior to the US-led invasion of Iraq, Latif had engineered chemical weapons for Saddam Hussein. For his efforts, he was made the five of diamonds in the US military's "Most Wanted Iraqi" playing cards. In homage to Latif's infamous past, Cudjoe's briefcase contained the Iraqi's fee in uncut diamonds.

At twenty-two, Tanu Baafi was the youngest member of the eight-man security detail aboard the helicopter. The reedy lieutenant's decade-long climb through the ranks began when he was conscripted as a boy during the civil war that followed Cudjoe's coup. One of the few boy soldiers to reach manhood, he had made a profession out of the only skill he possessed.

It was the height of the dry season and the tall grasses of the vast northern savanna stood sun-bleached and brittle as straw. The flight ended at a large rectangular clearing of scorched earth. Baafi studied the scene outside the porthole window as the helicopter slowed to a hover. Several khaki-colored military trucks lined one side of the clearing, showing at least forty soldiers. Two large, open-sided tents formed a command post with an array of communications and weather gear. A windsock fluttered limply, indicating a mild wind blowing out of the Sahara.

A lone transport stood at the far southern end of the clearing—a Bofors FH77 Archer. It was an articulated, six-wheeled truck consisting of a four-man armored crew cabin in front and a 155mm, self-loading Howitzer turret in the rear. The barrel of the field cannon stood at a high elevation, aimed at an unseen target several miles distant.

The helicopter landed in the center of a large H painted on the ground on the opposite side of the clearing from the Archer. Baafi and half the security detail deplaned first, followed by Cudjoe and Latif, and the remainder of the men.

The general in charge of the field test and several members of his staff snapped to attention as their commander-in-chief approached. Cudjoe parted his security detail and saluted the officers, then turned his attention to the general.

"Report," Cudjoe commanded.

"Sir, the weather conditions are ideal for the test. The forecast for the next few hours is warm and dry with clear skies and light winds out of the north. There is no sign of the Harmattan."

Cudjoe nodded, thankful to avoid an encounter with the dry, dusty sandstorms that raged out of the Sahara this time of year. "And the munitions?"

"The gunnery crew reports that the weapon is fully operational and ready for the test. Three 155mm rounds have been loaded with fuses set for an airburst fifty meters above the target."

"Does that meet your specifications?" Cudjoe asked Latif.

"Yes, Excellency, it does."

Cudjoe returned his attention to the general. "And the target?"

"We've established a wide perimeter around the target area and the troops have been equipped with protective gear for the test."

"Good," Cudjoe said. "You may proceed."

The Safolese leader and his guest were shown to seats beneath an open tent with a clear view of the Archer and an array of large LED screens displaying terrain and weather data. After the flight, Cudjoe preferred to stand, locking his gaze on the long, slender cannon pointed skyward.

The Archer shuddered as the Howitzer roared and the first shell flew into the air. The turret adjusted slightly for the second round, then the third. In a mere thirteen seconds, three volleys arced across the savanna.

THE WOMAN DID NOT hear the Archer's thunder as she sat weaving a basket, but noticed that the many birds that populated the massive acacia tree had suddenly grown silent. She then heard a faint whistling growing louder like an angry kettle on the fire.

There was an explosion overhead, followed by a puff of smoke that appeared above the treetop. The birds scattered as tiny metal fragments rattled through the branches. After two more explosions marked the sky, the three smoky clouds formed a triangle over the small village. Some of the woman's neighbors looked up from their chores while others ran for shelter.

As she watched the wisps of smoke, the woman detected the aroma of bitter almonds. Several birds fell from the sky and landed nearby, their bodies racked by death spasms. The woman pressed the fabric of her *bou-bou* tight against her mouth and nose, praying for the nightmarish scene to end. Her breathing came in panicked bursts and her heart raced inside her chest. Dizzy and nauseated, the woman collapsed against the trunk of the tree.

★

CUDJOE WATCHED THE AIRBURSTS over the village on the monitors. Remote cameras fitted with telephoto lenses captured the scene, including the deaths of many birds as they attempted to flee the upper limbs of a large acacia tree.

"Baafi!" Cudjoe called out.

Baafi approached and snapped to attention. "Yes, sir."

"You are a good observer. You will be my eyes," Cudjoe said. "The general is sending a squad of men to inspect the village. Go with them and report back to me."

"Yes, sir."

Baafi collected a radio headset and joined the rest of the survey team as they boarded a truck for the test site. Kijiji was only a few kilometers downwind from the Archer, so the heavy truck closed the distance on the rutted path quickly.

One kilometer north of the village, the truck stopped so the occupants could don chemical suits. Baafi felt his body temperature rising inside the suit as he secured the seals around his wrists and cinched a web belt with a holstered pistol around his waist. He took a few slow, deep breaths to suppress a growing sensation of claustrophobia.

The truck stopped just north of the village and the survey team covered the remaining distance on foot. The village was a typical collection of cylindrical buildings with conical thatched roofs joined by low walls to form a compound. In a noticeable break from tradition, no one came out to meet them.

Baafi heard nothing but the rustling of the multilayered chemical suit and his own breathing. The wind barely fluttered the leaves of a large acacia tree. All else was still and silent.

He followed the team into a large building that served as the entry into the compound. Inside, they found an elderly man, likely the village chief, lying on the ground. His eyes were rolled back such that only white was visible. Foamy spittle ran from his mouth.

More bodies lay inside the compound—adults and children and the livestock either dead or dying. The poison unleashed by the Iraqi engineer spared no one, not even the flies that feast on the newly dead. Baafi had seen death before and had on orders killed many, but the murder of this village felt evil.

The temperature inside Baafi's suit was climbing. With sweat beading across his forehead and soaking his uniform, he steadied himself against a doorway to counteract his growing light-headedness. As his vision cleared, he noticed the traditional mural painted around the opening. Though common to this region of Africa, intricate geometries on this doorway seemed impossibly familiar. His eyes swept back and forth across the design and he knew that he'd seen *this* pattern before.

One of the few memories Baafi retained from his abbreviated childhood was of his mother decorating the doorways of his village. He was perhaps five and his mother had taken a break from painting to get a drink of water. Imitating her, he had stuck his hand in a bowl of ocher paint and made a full handprint on the wall. His mother reprimanded him, but incorporated the mark he'd made into her design. The hidden handprint was their secret and only they could see it. Near the bottom of the right jamb, Baafi found his mark.

Baafi fled the courtyard, fearing that his suit had failed and that whatever had killed these people was beginning to affect him. He bent over, hands on his knees, gasping and overheated. Gradually, his heart rate returned to normal and he realized he wasn't dying. He then heard footsteps approaching from the village.

"You okay, man?" the squad medic asked, looking through Baafi's face shield.

"Yes, just getting hot."

"I'll be glad to get out of this suit, too, but not until we're clear of the area and hosed down. Understand?"

Baafi nodded. The medic patted him on the shoulder and returned to his work collecting blood samples from the victims. Baafi had seen enough of the village and would remain outside its walls. He spotted the acacia tree and felt that eerie sense of déjà vu again.

As a boy, he and his friends had climbed in a tree like this one. To see such a great living thing amid so much death seemed comforting. He found himself drawn toward it. Baafi was only a short distance away when he spotted the woman seated at the base of the tree. A partially woven basket having tumbled from her lap, she lay back against the trunk with both hands holding the cloth of her dress against her mouth and nose.

Baafi squatted in front of the woman and saw that she was not breathing. Gently, he lowered her hands into her lap and pulled the printed cloth of her *boubou* away from her face. Though the years and grief over the loss of a son had left their mark, he instantly recognized his mother's face. And the lies of his mother's death and the razing of his village by Dutannuru rebels were laid bare.

# 2

VICTORY OR DEATH

The letters flowed from the fat tip of a black marker, the indelible ink bleeding into the camouflage fabric stretched taut over the combat helmet. Ross Egan peered over the shoulder of the young man who carefully rendered the block letters onto the brow of the helmet on his lap. So intent was the soldier on his task that he failed to notice his audience.

" 'These are the times that try men's souls,' " Egan quoted.

Upon hearing the unique sound of English spoken with a flat mid-American accent, the soldier bolted to his feet and in a fluid motion donned his helmet and snapped a crisp salute.

"At ease, Sergeant," Egan said reassuringly. "I'm a civilian."

"Orders, sir. You are *bwana*—master of the power plant."

"I'm just the guy who keeps the lights on, but if it will make you feel better," Egan stiffened his stance to offer his best approximation of a salute. "Now, at ease."

The soldier set his feet shoulder width apart but remained ramrod straight.

"May I see your helmet?" Egan asked.

"Yes, sir."

With both hands, the soldier removed his helmet and placed it in Egan's hands. The engineer read the brave words in the waning daylight and pondered their meaning.

" 'Remember the Alamo,' sir."

"Hmm?" Egan responded absently.

"William Barret Travis. These were his words."

"They were indeed. And like you, Travis borrowed them from another soldier locked in a desperate struggle for liberty." Egan handed the helmet back. "Why are these words now yours?"

"I fought in the last war, the one that split my country."

Egan studied the soldier's face. "How old are you?"

"Twenty-three."

"You would have been just a boy"—Egan quickly reconciled the two facts—"a boy soldier."

"I was from a small village in what is now the demilitarized zone. Early in the war, Cudjoe's men raided it in retribution for our support of the rebels. All the women of the village, my mother and my sisters, were raped and murdered. My father, the village elders, and other men were forced to watch before they too were executed. I was taken with the other boys and made to—"

Egan held up his hand to halt the soldier's painful narrative. "I know what they made you boys do. There is a special place in Hell reserved for the Glorious Leader."

The soldier nodded. "I am a husband. My wife has just given me a son. I gladly risk my life to protect theirs."

"I understand."

Egan extended his hand to the soldier, who accepted it with a strong, firm grip. Though more than twenty years his senior, Egan knew both the man's pain and his motivation.

"Victory or death," the soldier offered.

"For us all."

Egan left the soldier to his duties and resumed his walk around the grounds of the power plant. He knew every square foot of the place, having rebuilt much of it from the ground up. The facility had been badly damaged in the civil war, stripped of all but the heaviest pieces of equipment and abandoned by Cudjoe's retreating forces. The same was true of all the territory ceded by Safo—lands that emerged as the Republic of Dutannuru.

During the 1960s, the Safolese government dammed the Umoja River and built the 300-megawatt power plant. The plant stood near the tip of a peninsula formed by a sharp bend in the river. Unfortunately, from the Dutannuru point of view, the plant was on the wrong side of the river.

The agreement that ended the civil war divided the two nations down the center of the Umoja River. The power plant, which was the primary source of electrical power for Dutannuru, stood squarely on Safo's side of the river. Over Cudjoe's strenuous objections, the diplomats straightened the border at the river bend and severed ten square kilometers of the jungle peninsula in Dutannuru's favor. As the Safolese army withdrew from the ceded peninsula, they left nothing behind but wreckage.

A pair of fences ringed the power plant, a ten-foot-high electrified inner fence to deter human intrusion surrounded by a five-foot-high livestock version to ward off jungle fauna. Due to a recent spate of incidents along the Dutannuru-Safo border, the army's corps of engineers had augmented the power plant's defenses with fortified gun emplacements. Combat troops were now in place and ready should open hostilities commence.

The dull thump of rotor blades grew louder until a military helicopter appeared over the power plant.

"Sir," the soldier he'd just spoken to called out as he ran toward Egan. "Yes?"

"Orders, sir. I'm to take you to the helipad. You have a visitor."

"All right."

Egan kept pace with the soldier as they briskly strode across the open yard. An officer dressed in fatigues emerged from the helicopter, followed by a pair of khaki-clad civilians. Both toted shoulder bags, the woman of the pair protectively cradling a digital camera. The trio hunched down beneath the whirling blades and trotted out toward them.

As they closed the distance, the officer returned the salute offered by Egan's escort and dismissed the soldier before turning to the engineer. Egan's gaze darted from the officer to the civilians. From beneath the brim of the woman's jungle hat, he noted the hint of a distantly familiar smile.

"Niki?" Egan shouted over the din as his mind put a name to the lovely face.

Clear of the rotors, Niki Adashi stood and nodded, her face beaming. Slender and nearly as tall as Egan, she threw her free arm around his neck in a friendly embrace.

"You remember me!" Niki said happily.

"It hasn't been that long," Egan replied.

"Please come with me," the officer said, interrupting the reunion.

Egan nodded and they quickly moved away from the helipad.

"It is an honor to meet you, sir," the officer said once they were inside the command post. "I am Major Opoku. I apologize for my abrupt arrival."

"Not necessary, Major," Egan replied, "but why are you ferrying out visitors with God knows what about to happen?"

"Orders, sir. These people represent the international media."

From the tone of Opoku's voice, Egan knew the man was less than thrilled with the idea of shepherding reporters into a likely battle zone.

"I'm Edward Turcott, freelance journalist with the *Times*," the man said as he thrust his hand toward Egan. "I gather from your meeting outside that you are already acquainted with Ms. Adashi."

"I am," Egan replied.

"Excuse me, Major," Turcott interjected. "I know you gentlemen have business, but the daylight is waning and we'd like to have a look around before dark."

Niki stood quietly by Turcott, holding a long-lens camera in the crook of her arm the way a big game hunter would have cradled a Holland & Holland .375 Royal Deluxe.

"And I thought you came halfway around the world just to visit an old friend," Egan said to Niki.

"Sadly, no," Niki said. "I am here in the event that Cudjoe attacks. President Mensah wishes the world to know."

"I can think of no one better than you to capture Dutannuru's plight," Egan said. "I assume your selection for this assignment wasn't purely by chance?"

"Like you, I place my trust in higher powers," Niki replied with a knowing smile.

"As I said, I'd like to have a look around," Turcott reiterated, perturbed. "President Mensah assured me that Ms. Adashi and I would have full access to this facility."

"Your access is not quite as full as you think," Egan replied. "Talk to whomever you like, but you cannot enter or photograph the interior of the powerhouse."

"Why not?" Turcott asked.

"National security," Opoku interjected tersely. "If you take any unau-
thorized photographs or enter restricted areas, you will be imprisoned."

"You're joking," Turcott snorted haughtily.

"I am not," Opoku replied stonily. "Go now."

Turcott retreated from the trailer quickly, thankful to be out of
Opoku's sight. Niki shared a quick glance with Egan and an unspoken
promise to talk when they had an opportunity.

"I can't believe Mensah has you running a press tour," Egan said once
the door closed behind Niki.

"He kills two birds with one stone. You are the primary reason I am
here. The Embassy of the United States has issued an evacuation notice
to all of its citizens in Dutannuru. President Mensah has ordered that you
be brought to the capital and evacuated with your fellow countrymen."

"He knows better than that."

"The President warned me that you might be difficult." Opoku turned
to the duty officer. "Do you have the secure line I requested?"

"Yes, sir. You can take the call in my office."

Opoku led Egan into a small room at the end of the trailer. A light
on the multiline phone blinked expectantly. Opoku picked up the phone
and identified himself, then waited. After a moment, the major's posture
stiffened as if a superior officer had entered the room.

"Yes, Mr. President. He is with me."

Opoku listened for a brief moment before offering the handset to
Egan.

"Mr. President," Egan said warmly.

"Ross, your government has chartered a plane that will depart the
capital in one hour. I think you should go."

"Is that why you sent Niki?"

"No, but I will not complain if her presence results in your achieving
a longer life. I do not wish you to suffer the fate of Archimedes. You are
too valuable, my friend."

Egan recalled the murder of the brilliant Greek mathematician during
the chaos that followed the fall of Syracuse to the Romans during the
Second Punic War.

"This is as much my fight as yours," Egan countered.

"And the first thing Cudjoe will attack is *your* power plant."

"We always knew that would be the case—plus it just irks the Illustrious Leader that we can keep the lights on and he can't. All the more reason for me to stay. And if Cudjoe does take this plant, he'll find it just as he left it."

"I hope it does not come to that."

"You and me both, but if there's no other choice..."

"Very well. Give Major Opoku this phrase: *Mtoto shupavu sana.*"

Egan smiled and repeated the phrase. Opoku nodded and left the command post without him.

"Maggie used to call me that," Egan said.

"She was right, and you remain a *stubborn child.*"

Egan heard the rustle of papers over the phone.

"I have received some new intelligence," Mensah continued. "Satellite images from just a few hours ago show Cudjoe has moved additional forces into the border region near the power plant. There are staging areas for armored troop carriers and attack helicopters. My generals believe the attack will come soon."

"The US government is providing you information?" Egan asked, incredulous.

"We acquired the images from a private firm."

Egan detected the bitter undertone in Mensah's reply. When the prospect of a second war over Dutannuru had emerged, many of the world's leading political figures made speeches urging dialogue and brokered negotiations. Shuttle diplomacy by the globetrotting American Secretary of State resulted in little more than a well-staged photo opportunity for the saber-rattling dictator. A UN resolution denouncing Safo's increasingly hostile stance toward its smaller neighbor was killed by nations that were quietly trading arms for access to the vast natural resources of the repressive people's state.

"There was a time when the United States stood shoulder to shoulder with nations like Dutannuru in defense of liberty."

"A pragmatic approach is the current political fashion," Mensah offered. "And the pragmatists believe Dutannuru's days are numbered."

"Pragmatist is just a polite way of saying pessimist. I believe in the people of Dutannuru."

"I, too, believe in my people. And in you. May God be with you in the coming storm."

"May He be with us all, Mr. President."

Egan left the command post and resumed his tour of the grounds around the power plant. The automatic lights that normally flickered on at sunset remained off—the facility and its defenders cloaked themselves in the jungle darkness. Above him, a clear, moonless sky sparkled with the tiny lights of distant stars.

The younger soldiers were restless, eager for snippets of news, rumors, and speculation about the looming conflict. Veterans of the last war knew from experience that the future would take care of itself and that a soldier must concern himself with the present. Those who were off-duty ate or slept, knowing both those activities become elusive in battle. Others ritually inspected and cleaned their weapons and equipment to ensure all was in peak working condition.

The jungle takes on a different character at night, and the presence of so many men had disrupted the natural rhythm of the nocturnal creatures. Darkness and silence enhanced the palpable sense of anticipation.

Egan's iPhone vibrated silently in his belt holder. He checked the screen and read the text message: **Look Up.**

He holstered the phone and scanned the sky. The message was an application that he'd written to text him whenever the International Space Station was passing overhead. He remembered a cool, July night in his childhood when his parents woke him and sat with him in front of a grainy black-and-white television to watch Neil Armstrong and Buzz Aldrin walk on the moon. He had retained a passion for space exploration to this day.

Egan heard the metallic click of a camera shutter.

"Wishing on a star?" Niki asked, her face subtly up-lit by the faint glow of the camera's LCD screen.

"Not quite," Egan replied, his gaze still fixed upward.

Then he saw it. The bright object streaked out of the northwest, moving diagonally across the sky.

"Look there," Egan said, pointing skyward.

"A meteor?" Niki asked.

"A space station," Egan replied.

"With war so close, it is hard to imagine that people can accomplish something so extraordinary. It is very fast."

"Has to be," Egan offered, "or it would quickly come crashing to Earth."

"Might not be such a bad thing," Turcott opined as he uploaded a story from his iPad. "I think the manned space program is a colossal waste of time and money."

"So says the man whose livelihood depends on technologies born from man's hopeful desire 'to slip the surly bonds of earth' and 'touch the face of God.' "

"Touché," Turcott conceded, "and very poetic."

"My wife was a great reader of poetry. I guess some of it rubbed off on me. *High Flight* is one of my favorites."

Niki laughed fondly. "She described her attempts to expose you to literature as *cultural diffusion*. I think of her often. She was a good woman."

Egan nodded. "Our time together was too brief, but I'm thankful for it."

They watched the ISS hurtle across the night sky until it disappeared behind the distant jungle canopy. The pointed tip of a crescent moon emerged over the eastern horizon.

"And may that be the only thing we see lighting up the sky tonight," Egan said. "Though it'll mean you wasted a trip out here."

"Wars are like cabs in Manhattan," Turcott said. "There's always another one just around the corner."

"I took some interesting pictures and met an old friend," Niki offered. "However it turns out this trip will not be fruitless for me."

"Do you shoot landscapes?" Egan asked.

"If I like the scenery," Niki replied.

"Come with me."

Egan led Niki and Turcott toward the power plant. The complex of buildings seemed eerily quiet in the darkness. They skirted the main buildings and approached a guarded gate. After a quick check of his credentials, Egan escorted the reporters onto the upper deck of the dam. The lake formed by the dam spread lengthwise to the east. To the west, a steep cliff face of concrete plunged to the river valley below. He stopped at a point near the center of the dam.

"Oh my," Niki gasped.

From this vantage, the thin sickle moon hung low in the sky over the far end of the lake, reflecting perfectly in the placid water. Niki unfolded a tripod and quickly calculated the settings required to capture the image.

"That is what really should have brought you here," Egan said. "Not another war waged by a murderous parasite."

"Not a fan of Kwame Cudjoe?" Turcott asked.

"Hardly," Egan replied. "The thug seized power in a coup that threw his country into civil war and led to the deaths of tens of thousands. He took three-quarters of the land along with the major oil fields, mines, and industry, leaving Dutannuru with next to nothing. A decade later, Cudjoe has nationalized everything, his people are starving, tens of thousands more are dead, and his nation is a total basket case. And right next door, the spit of land he left in ruins is fast becoming the economic lion of Africa. This isn't a war—it's a heist. And the cop who used to patrol this beat is nowhere to be found."

"If war comes again, do you think it will go badly for Dutannuru?" Niki asked.

"Wars rarely go well when an enemy is massing on your border."

"If you're an American, why are you still here?" Turcott asked. "That helicopter we arrived in was sent to whisk you away from this place before hostilities commence."

"My wife came here with the Peace Corps when all of this was Safo. The government then was ineffective and riddled with corruption, but foreign aid was welcome and she fell in love with the people."

As he spoke, Egan watched Niki patiently work her camera. Sensing him, she paused.

"I was still a girl when I met his wife," she explained to Turcott. "Maggie became part of our community, like family. I miss her to this day."

Egan nodded. "Bettering the lives of the people here was my wife's calling. After we married, I returned with her and this is where we made our home. That's why I refuse to leave."

Niki finished shooting the moonlit landscape and detached her camera from the tripod. Ripples on the far end of the lake disturbed the reflection, wakes radiating from the black silhouettes moving in a straight line toward the dam. She saw that Egan had noticed the incoming boats as well.

"Are those boats Safolese?" Turcott asked.

"Don't know," Egan answered, "but it's probably not a good idea to wait here to find out."

Niki quickly stowed her tripod and they all headed back the way they came. The moon illuminated the plant buildings and cast long, dark shadows.

"What are you hiding in there?" Turcott asked casually.

"Nothing," Egan replied with a hint of evasion.

"Then why all the security? I've been inside power plants before, if that's your worry. I did a piece on the Three Rivers Gorge project in China a while back."

"That's cutting-edge hydro. What's in there isn't nearly as impressive."

Turcott eyed him suspiciously. "When you say it like that, you just make me more curious."

"We all need a little mystery in our lives."

As they neared the end of the dam, a figure climbed onto the walkway and strode toward them. It was Major Opoku.

"Ah, I have found you," Opoku said, relieved.

"I thought you returned to the capital," Egan said.

"I volunteered for duty here. I am now on the general's staff."

"I'm sure he's glad to have you."

"If war comes to Dutannuru here, then this is where I must be."

"Spoken like a patriot, Major," Egan said warmly. "And speaking of war, we spotted some boats on the east end of the lake heading this way."

"Safolese patrol boats. We are monitoring them as well as troop movements along the border. The helicopter that brought us here," Opoku said to the reporters, "has been redeployed. We have confirmed reports that Cudjoe ordered a test of chemical munitions on a small village in northern Safo earlier today. Many were killed."

"Shouldn't these two be evacuated?" Egan asked.

"Like you, they volunteered to be here and the helicopter was required elsewhere. Cudjoe may use chemical shells against us. We have protective suits, helmets, and body armor for you all."

"Cheery thought," Turcott offered.

"Thank you," Egan added, grateful for the consideration.

"I also bring a request from the general. He asks if you would address his men."

"Why me?" Egan asked, taken aback, "I'm just a civilian, and a foreigner to boot."

"You were part of the First Council," Opoku countered. "Your role in creating Dutannuru is well known. Words you wrote are taught to our children. The general heard you speak at the First Council. He believes you are a wise and honest man. With war so close, he asks that you speak to his soldiers. In your words, he believes they will find truth and courage."

"I would be honored," Egan said.

"Then all of you, please follow me to the command post."

Opoku's arm seemed in constant motion, saluting the junior officers and enlisted men they encountered while crossing the compound. Niki and Turcott both noted that the men accorded Egan equal respect.

"The general asks that you speak at nineteen hundred hours," Opoku said as they reached the command post. "He apologizes for making his request on such short notice."

"Unnecessary. I just need a little time to collect my thoughts."

"Of course," Opoku said. "Use the duty office. You will speak from there."

"May we join you?" Niki asked.

"Sure," Egan answered.

Opoku left Egan with Niki and Turcott in the duty office. He provided them with cold sodas and promised to return when it was closer to the time of his address to the troops.

"So just what are you?" Turcott asked Egan as he settled onto a small couch beside Niki. "One of Dutannuru's Founding Fathers?"

"More like a founding friend of the family," Egan replied as he sat down behind the desk. "I advised President Mensah when the council drafted the country's constitution."

"He's too modest," Niki protested. "The name of Ross Egan is honored in Dutannuru."

"How well do you know Mensah?" Turcott asked.

"He was godfather to my son."

"I see."

Niki reviewed the images stored in her camera's memory. Most were of young soldiers preparing to shoulder the burden of war.

*How many would pay the price of this war in maimed bodies and lost lives?* she wondered. *What would be the cost?*

Niki reached her photographs of the moonrise over the lake. Turcott glanced at the beautiful images.

"You were right," Turcott admitted. "We should've come here for the scenery."

"That and the people," Egan offered.

"Are they really all that different?"

"No, but that's the point. Where it really matters, the people of Dutannuru are the same as those back in the States or anywhere else in the world. They all want to live peaceful and productive lives."

"Then why is Dutannuru going to war?" Turcott asked.

"Dutannuru is not *going* to war," Egan answered. "War is *coming* to Dutannuru."

"But can't they negotiate with Cudjoe?" Turcott pressed further. "End this thing before it starts?"

"Can you negotiate with a burglar as he's kicking in your door?" Egan countered.

" 'All war represents a failure of diplomacy,' " Turcott replied.

"Bet you learned that Tony Benn chestnut in some political theory class," Egan said with a chuckle. "Was your prof a tweedy Marxist?"

"Progressive feminist, actually."

"Same difference."

"Diplomacy is a tactic of war," Turcott offered. " 'Supreme excellence consists of breaking an enemy's resistance without fighting.' "

"Sun Tzu—I see you're up on the classics," Egan said. "Hitler skillfully employed both diplomacy and blitzkrieg in the pursuit of his ambitions. This is true throughout history."

"So tell me, what is war?" Turcott asked sharply.

"Are you familiar with the Ten Commandments?" Egan asked.

"Of course, but how do they relate to war?"

"They provide context. Oh, and for reference, I'm using the variation where only the first three commandments are religious and the rest are civil."

Turcott nodded that he understood and Egan continued.

"Offensive wars are based on breaking the Tenth, Seventh, and Fifth Commandments, in that order. It starts when the leadership of one nation covets the wealth or property of another, breaking the Tenth. Acting on this desire with the use or threat of force is theft, breaking the Seventh. The aggressor breaks the Fifth when it uses lethal force to take what it desires. Cudjoe's actions follow this pattern. Now, there can be pretext and antagonism between rival nations, but when you distill an offensive war down to its essence, you always find a thief trying to steal something."

"Wasn't the US invasion of Iraq an offensive war?" Turcott asked.

"No, it was an offensive action taken in the context of a larger war, like D-Day. A better analogy might be the use of atomic bombs on Japan—both were hotly debated actions taken with the sole intent of protecting American lives. The United States didn't start the Second World War, but it did launch a number of offensive actions to end it and restore the peace. Along the same lines, Israel has launched what some have called unprovoked attacks on its neighbors in order to prevent those neighbors from acquiring nuclear weapons. These were in fact offensive actions in an ongoing defensive war that has existed since Israel's founding. That is the right of the aggrieved nation." Egan set his elbows on the desk and leaned forward. "Should Safo attack, Dutannuru must drive them back and accept nothing less than unconditional surrender."

"Do you see why the general asked him to speak?" Niki asked Turcott. "Now, will you please give the man a moment to prepare his thoughts."

Turcott conceded the point and returned to his article. Egan gave Niki a grateful wink, then turned pensive. As she uploaded her images to the press pool back in the nation's capital, she found her eyes drawn to Egan's face. He was lost in thought, oblivious to her observation. The years, she decided, had been kind to him.

Turcott, too, wondered what kind of man he'd stumbled upon in a place he didn't know existed just a few days ago.

# 3

"IN THIS LAND, GOD created the ancestors of all mankind."

Egan's clear tenor voice resonated from the two-way radios carried by the soldiers defending the power plant. He wore a wireless headset and spoke from behind the desk. Adashi and Turcott sat silently on the couch. Opoku stood in the doorway.

"And in that act of creation, he endowed us all with certain rights that no one can take from us. Greater minds than mine summarized the most sacred of these rights as life, liberty, and the pursuit of happiness.

"A decade ago, the people of this land paid a terrible price to reclaim their patrimony. As was their right, they threw off the burden of a failed and corrupt government that had bankrupted the nation. As was their right, they rejected the tyrant who murdered his way to power and made war on those who resisted him.

"Those brave and hopeful rebels, who sacrificed all for the promise of providing a better world for themselves and their descendants, knew that terrible civil war could only end for them in victory or in death. There could be no surrender. They would accept no chains. The people of this land chose to live free or die.

"And many did die to restore the freedoms now enjoyed by the people of Dutannuru. We owe a debt of honor to those patriots, a blessed obligation to defend that which they redeemed with their blood.

"The memory of that civil war remains fresh among those who survived it; all but the first generation born in liberty bear the scars of that conflict. That war left one people divided into two nations. Those who toiled in the warm light of liberty took what was left them and prospered. Their kin, blessed with far greater natural resources, struggle to survive as the fruits of their labor are squandered for the glorification of a madman. The only difference between the people of these two nations is on which side of the Umoja River they stand.

"This unnatural division is the work left undone, a task we had hoped to complete in peace but are now forced to undertake in war. The army massing on our border is not the enemy—they are *our family*, and they are tormented by a great devil. What comes is a war of two nations, but one people. Dutannuru does not seek this war, but will fight it if we must. We will fight for all that we hold dear, and not just to protect our freedom, but to win back theirs. The only way this war can end is with *one* nation.

"For all Dutannuru—*Victory or Death!*"

"LISTEN TO THEM," OPOKU said proudly.

The defenders of the Umoja power plant responded to Egan's address with a roar of approval. Like the troops at Trenton and the Alamo, the defenders' courage found voice in chanting the famous motto—*Victory or Death.*

"Quite a speech," Turcott said flatly as he made some notes.

"It was a beautiful speech," Niki countered as she snapped another photo of Egan seated behind the desk.

Egan waved her off and removed the headset. "I just told them the truth."

"That is why I asked you to address my men," a voice boomed from outside the room.

Opoku stepped aside and cleared the way for General Darko. A squat man with the build of a water buffalo, he crossed the room beaming and extended a beefy hand to Egan.

"You touched their hearts," Darko said. "Your words are stronger than any fear of the unknown. I thank you."

Egan stood and shook the general's hand. "I'm glad to help."

"We expect the attack will come soon," Darko said, turning serious. "I am going to visit with my men. Will you come with me?"

"Of course."

"May we join you?" Niki asked, camera in hand.

The general nodded and led the way out with Opoku and the others in tow.

# 4

THE NEXT HOURS PASSED quickly as Egan and Darko spoke with small groups of men positioned around the power plant. The soldiers, who would likely take the brunt of the expected attack, seemed both nervous and resolute, knowing their fight was in the service of a greater good.

"You've attracted quite a following," Turcott said to Egan as they walked toward the next group of soldiers.

"Must be my fifteen minutes of fame."

Between stops, Opoku remained at General Darko's side, quietly relaying orders from an incoming report to his commanding officer.

"That is very interesting," Darko said, turning to face Egan. "The government is broadcasting your speech nationally."

"You're kidding," Egan replied.

"I am not. President Mensah liked what you said very much and he wished all of Dutannuru to hear your words."

After Opoku's two-way squawked, he switched the radio to send-receive mode. He wore an earpiece and throat mike under his helmet, so what little they heard of the conversation was one-sided jargon.

"What is it, Opoku?" Darko asked on completion of the report.

"Sir," Opoku replied, "activity along the border has increased significantly within the last twenty minutes."

"Have they crossed?" Darko asked.

"No, and the reports we're getting are confusing. There doesn't appear to be any coordination..." Opoku paused as another report came in.

"Sir, a Safolese helicopter is hovering at the border requesting permission to approach and land here for the purpose of parley."

"This is very odd," Darko mused. "Do we have a visual on this helicopter?"

"Yes, sir. It is unescorted and running with full lights on."

"Is it carrying any weapons or external tanks?"

Opoku relayed the question and waited a moment for a reply.

"Our forward observer reports the helicopter is a large military transport," Opoku said. "No weapons are visible."

"Is there any further information on the chemical weapon they tested? How it was delivered?"

"No, sir."

Darko considered all that he'd heard for a moment.

"If they wish to talk, I will let them talk. Permission granted. Tell the Safolese that we will provide an armed escort to accompany them from the border to this facility. They are to fly in formation with our escort, and they are to keep their communications open and maintain contact. Inform them that their escort is under orders to fire on them should they deviate from their instructions. All troops are to remain on full alert."

"Yes, sir."

Opoku moved off to begin issuing orders to the groups affected by the inbound helicopter.

"Might this be a ruse?" Niki asked Egan.

"Darko's not buying it," Egan replied. "Cudjoe pulled a fake parley once during the last war and killed a lot of people."

Egan, Niki, and Turcott followed the general back to the command post to await the arrival of the Safolese representative. Opoku kept pace with the general, feeding the commanding officer a steady stream of updates.

The Safolese helicopter and its escort of two Dutannuru attack helicopters followed a course that routed them downwind of the power plant on their approach. The huge Mil Mi-26P dwarfed its escorts, causing Egan to wonder if the helipad could accommodate the aircraft's forty-meter length. It hovered over the pad as floodlights washed it in search of weapons. Satisfied that the helicopter posed no visible threat, Darko granted permission for it to land.

The helicopter descended slowly, the pilot aware of the weapons trained on the aircraft should he make any suspicious moves. He landed it lightly and powered down the twin Lotarev turboshaft engines. The escort helicopters remained aloft, hovering in position to act if necessary. Slowly, the long rotors wound to a stop. As the dust settled, the emblem near the nose of the aircraft became clearly visible.

"Is that Cudjoe's helicopter?" Darko asked.

"Intel confirms that the markings match those of the helicopter assigned to transporting the Safolese head of state," Opoku reported.

"This makes no sense at all," Egan said absently.

"How so?" Niki asked, still snapping photos of the idle aircraft.

"There is no reason to believe Cudjoe is inside that helicopter, and I can't imagine his handpicked flight crew would decide to defect on the eve of war."

"Maybe Cudjoe *is* in there and he just wants to talk," Turcott said.

"God, I hope not," Egan shot back. "That windbag gives marathon speeches at the drop of a hat. It's possible he's sent an emissary to offer us a chance to surrender the power plant now and walk away without a bloodbath. But I just can't believe he thinks that Dutannuru would simply roll over."

The helicopter's forward door opened and the pilot descended the steps. He was in a flight suit with his helmet tucked under one arm and the other clearly visible. The holster for his sidearm was empty. He took a few steps away from the door and stopped, squinting in the bright light at the command post.

Darko motioned for Opoku and a pair of armed soldiers to accompany him and the four strode toward the pilot. On seeing the rank insignia on Darko's uniform, the pilot snapped to attention and saluted.

"At ease," Darko replied as he returned the salute. "Why are you here, Captain?"

Egan could not hear the exchange but found it odd when the general and Opoku both turned in his direction. A moment later, one of the soldiers jogged over.

"Sir," the soldier said, "the general requests your presence."

Egan nodded and followed the soldier onto the helipad. Without asking permission, Niki impetuously joined him.

"You sure you want to do this?" Egan asked in a half whisper.

"What's the worst that could happen?"

Egan arched an eyebrow at her but offered no reply as they neared the men standing on the helipad.

"This is the man who made the speech?" the pilot asked, surprised to see a Caucasian face.

"Yes," Darko replied firmly.

"Very well." The pilot cocked his head toward the helicopter and nodded.

A moment later, the rear door of the helicopter opened and three men in military uniforms slowly filed out. Like the pilot, they were unarmed and held their hands up at shoulder level as they spaced themselves alongside the helicopter. The braids on their uniforms indicated the men were part of an elite unit.

Niki gasped, but continued taking pictures when a fourth man emerged from the helicopter into the light. He was tall and thin and dressed like the others except that his uniform was disheveled and bloodstained. He walked purposefully toward them, arms hanging loosely from his sides, but unlike the others he was armed. In his right hand, he carried a machete, its blade blackened with dried blood. A small plastic cooler hung from his left.

The soldiers accompanying Darko trained their rifles on the man, who halted a safe distance from the group. He looked directly at Egan.

"Are you the man who made the speech, the man who said that we are one people?"

"I am," Egan replied.

The man's jaw tightened and he seemed on the verge of tears.

"I—" the man said, struggling to keep his voice even, "heard you."

The man set the cooler on the ground and dropped onto one knee. With his head deeply bowed, he held out the machete in his open palms. Unsure what to do, Egan turned to Darko, who nodded that he should accept the offering. Egan approached the man cautiously, hoping the soldiers still had their weapons ready in case the man suddenly attacked.

As Egan reached for the machete, he noted the man's hands were trembling. They steadied when Egan removed the blade, as if relieved of a terrible burden.

"For the people of Safo," the man said, "I surrender to our Dutannuru kinsmen."

Egan studied the bloody weapon and the kneeling man awaiting a response.

"On what terms and on whose authority do you speak?" Darko interjected.

"General," Egan replied, "I believe he speaks as the leader of Safo."

Darko's eyes widened, incredulous that the young officer had somehow seized power.

"Are you the leader of Safo?" Egan asked softly.

The man nodded, his head still bowed.

"Please stand and tell us what has happened," Egan asked.

The man rose up, tears glistening on his face. He stood at ease with his arms behind his back, his gaze fixed on Egan.

"My name is Tanu Baafi," he began. "I was a member of the security detail protecting President Kwame Cudjoe. I led a coup against him and he is dead. I killed Cudjoe. I am now leader of Safo."

"Why did you kill Cudjoe?" Egan asked.

"Today, he tested a terrible weapon."

"We know. He used it on a village in the north."

Baafi nodded. "I went to that village. It killed everyone. He planned to use this weapon here, against you. Many would have died. The only way to stop Cudjoe was to kill him."

"We are grateful," Egan said, speaking in even, measured tones.

"Do you control the army?" Darko asked.

"I killed Cudjoe before he was to meet with his generals. I went in his place. Most of the generals accepted me as their commander. Those that did not were relieved of duty and imprisoned. The army has been ordered to withdraw from the border and return to base."

"Can you prove any of what you say?" Darko asked warily.

Baafi picked up the cooler and, cradling it in the crook of his left arm, opened the top.

"Our generals asked me the same question," Baafi replied. "This satisfied them."

Baafi tilted the open cooler slightly to reveal its contents. Inside was a pair of human heads.

"One is Cudjoe. The other, a man named Latif. Latif made the weapon for Cudjoe. Their bodies are inside the helicopter."

Egan had met Cudjoe once, before the civil war, and had seen the tyrant's distinctive face in the news many times during his brutal reign. One of the heads in the box had certainly belonged to Cudjoe. He stepped forward and closed the cooler lid, then offered his hand to Baafi.

"For your Dutannuru kinsmen, I accept your offer of surrender."

# 5

EGAN STOOD INSIDE THE cavernous powerhouse, staring through a gaping hole in the floor at the twisted remains of a seven-hundred-ton generator. Turbine Number 4 was twelve meters in diameter at its widest and, upright, equaled a three-story building in height. The turbine lay unnaturally on its side, ejected from its concrete and steel housing at the base of the Makola Dam.

"Can you fix it?" a woman's voice called out.

Egan looked down the length of the powerhouse and found his questioner at the near side of Turbine Number 2, walking through the wreckage toward him with a small retinue in tow. Maya Randell's petite frame was clad in tailored safari wear accented with an Emaa Da patterned kente cloth scarf. Her black hair was drawn back in a single tight braid emphasizing the almond shape of her face.

"S'cuse me?" Egan shouted back.

"You heard me. Can you fix it?"

"I can fix anything dats broke, ma'am," Egan thundered back, exaggerating the Yooper dialect of Michigan's Upper Peninsula, "but dat dere is definitely gonna cost ya more dan fifty bucks."

Maya laughed, recalling her first encounter with Egan. She and her husband Burton were both fresh out of graduate school and honeymooning across America when their VW camper hit a deer in Michigan's Upper Peninsula. Egan was a teenager at the time, working in his uncle's auto shop when the damaged vehicle was towed in. The accident occurred during the height of the summer tourist season and the hotels were full, so Egan's parents took in the stranded newlyweds for a week while their camper was being repaired.

The gangly redhead had impressed the Randells with his homemade computer and various electrical projects that rivaled thesis work by their fellow graduates from the Massachusetts Institute of Technology. They recognized Egan's potential and made a point to keep tabs on the promising young man.

Maya's bodyguards and personal assistant stopped several meters back and she closed the remaining distance alone. Egan stood a foot taller than Maya, so he bent slightly to meet her embrace and kissed her gently on the cheek. The young bride who became a tech boom billionaire embraced Egan as warmly as his family had greeted her so many years ago.

"Then it's a good thing I have a bit more money now than I did then."

"You and Burton made more in interest in the last ten seconds than that old camper cost new," Egan said as he released her.

"And that ratty old thing is still in our garage. Boys and their toys."

"Sentimental value," Egan said sympathetically. "So what brings you here?"

"Checking on my investment, of course," Maya replied. "But seriously, can you fix *that?*"

"I'm afraid Turbine Number Four is down for the count. One and Two are up and running now. Three and Five are damaged, but repairable. The dam wasn't damaged at all and the powerhouse can be put back in order in a few months."

"What happened?"

"I visited here a couple times back before the civil war and Number Four had problems from day one," Egan explained. "Last summer, it was down for some scheduled maintenance and a number of cracks and cavities in the turbine blades were repaired with welds. Routine stuff, but they didn't rebalance the turbine wheel afterward. The few workers who survived the accident said it was vibrating like crazy and then—*Bang!* The rotor came flying out of its seat and did all this. We'd heard rumors, but had no idea how bad the accident was. It knocked the plant off-line completely for several weeks and cut the Safo's total power supply by about a third. Most of the power made here goes to an aluminum plant, so that loss of power cut directly into Cudjoe's flow of hard currency."

"Cudjoe was going to make war on Dutannuru for energy?" Maya asked.

"He had a lot of reasons to go to war, but I think this accident pushed up his timetable. Mensah has made repairing this plant a national priority, now that this land is back to being one nation."

"I know," Maya said with a knowing smile. "He told me where I could find you."

"I leapt at the chance to get out of the capital. I can't go anywhere in public."

"That's what you get for being all white and freckly," Maya chided. "At least you finally have some gray to mute that red hair. Now I, on the other hand, am the perfect shade of mocha for this part of the world."

"You're about as African as I am Irish, and neither of us can walk the streets of the capital without getting mobbed."

"Ross, you are a national hero, or I should say, *international* hero."

Maya pulled a copy of the *Wall Street Journal* out of her shoulder bag and spread it out on a worktable. Above the fold was the now-iconic photograph of Egan accepting the Safolese surrender.

"This image is everywhere, and Niki Adashi is in very high demand."

"Good for her," Egan said.

"Good for *you*, and that's why I'm here. You've done some brilliant work in Dutannuru, and not just with electricity. This republic is the one bright spot on the African continent and your influence on its government is undeniable."

"Oh, I can deny it. Helping Mensah create an honest government here was Maggie's dream. She dedicated her life to these people."

"And you honored her sacrifice by helping make that dream a reality. Dutannuru was in as bad a shape as this place when it broke free, and now it enjoys one of the highest GDPs per capita in the world. The people here have jobs. Hell, they have food! All of the children are in school. And where else in Africa can you find a growing middle class? Every health statistic shows marked improvement. Dutannuru even has an immigration problem because folks in the neighboring countries know a good thing when they see it. And speaking of neighbors, when was the last time one sovereign nation asked to peacefully unite with another?"

"Mensah has provided wise leadership for his people."

"And a wise leader seeks good counsel," Maya said, "You've provided that to President Mensah. He told me that you've been invaluable to him in the unification and reconciliation process."

"*E Pluribus Unum*. There's a lot to be done," Egan admitted, "and he'll be missed when he steps down at the end of the year."

"There's talk in the legislature of you succeeding Mensah as president."

"That would be something," Egan said with a laugh. "Thankfully, the constitution of Dutannuru bars foreigners from elective office."

"No such prohibition against you exists in the United States."

Egan and Maya studied each other carefully for a moment. She then gave him a slight nod that she was serious.

"That's insane. I'm about as qualified as—"

"As *any* natural-born citizen of the United States who is over the age of thirty-five," Maya interjected. "Those are, of course, the bare minimum requirements for holding the highest office in the land. I prefer a resume of substantial accomplishments as well, but the last election taught us that it isn't a necessity. Article Two also contains a residency requirement, but my lawyers have reviewed the clause and have assured me it's not an obstacle."

"But I've never run for anything," Egan said.

"Neither did Washington or Eisenhower. They both won fame on the battlefield, but yours came through peace. Everything you've done for Dutannuru has prepared you to lead." Maya stabbed a slender finger at the newspaper photograph. "This defining act has thrust you onto the world stage and it forces us to rethink our plans. Our dream of bringing power to the people must grow beyond electricity or we waste an incredible opportunity to save our country before it's too late. The world needs the United States, and the United States needs you."

"This is the last thing I would ever have wanted."

"I know," Maya replied sympathetically, "but greatness has been thrust upon you. And it suits you."

Egan crossed his arms and stared down at the shattered turbine as he considered Maya's proposition. The engineers he'd trained could restore this power plant without him, while the country he'd helped found would soon elect new leadership. It was a time of change in Dutannuru, a perfect moment to step away and start something new.

"It's been a while since I last visited my folks," Egan said. "This is something I should talk over with them."

"Absolutely." Maya moved next to Egan and slipped her arm around his waist. With her free hand, she patted his forearm supportively. "But fair warning, I've already spoken with your father."

"And what did he say?"

"It's his idea. I just happen to agree with him."

"He is most definitely *not* a fan of the President," Egan said with a chuckle. "When do you need my answer?"

"You have a little time to think it over," Maya replied, "but soon. The election is less than two years off and we'll need every bit of that time to make a credible run."

"Fair enough," Egan said as he picked up the newspaper. "The President will be hard to beat—lousy leader or not, he is a savvy campaigner."

"And he's got all the unions, most of the press, and some major big-money backers solidly in his corner," Maya added. "It'll be tough, but he is definitely beatable."

Egan caught a hint of a conspiratorial smile on Maya's face, and her eyes sparkled with a glint of mischief.

"Why do I get the feeling you and that devious husband of yours already have an intriguing campaign strategy in mind?"

"The way to beat our President is to give him everything that he *thinks* he needs to win."

# 6

NIKI ADASHI STROLLED CONFIDENTLY across the elegant lobby of the Willard Hotel, the heels of her leather boots tapping lightly on the marble floor. She wore a stylish, full-length camel hair coat with a colorful scarf loosely wrapped over her head and a woven bag dangling from her arm. She was pulling on a pair of leather gloves when she spotted Egan seated by a window.

"Right on time," Egan said with a smile as he rose to greet her.

Niki offered a cheek and he gave her a friendly peck.

"This is not an event I wish to be fashionably late for," she replied. "And I must say you are looking very handsome this evening."

Egan, dressed in black-tie formal, nodded a thank you and slipped on a navy overcoat.

"Do you have the invitation?" Niki asked.

Egan patted his left breast pocket and felt the stiff embossed cardstock. "Right here."

They exited through the revolving door and out under the glass canopy protecting the hotel's Pennsylvania Avenue entrance. It was just past sunset and the temperature hovered in the high twenties under a clear evening sky. Egan offered his arm and the pair moved briskly up the street. Niki easily kept pace with his long-legged strides. On the opposite side of the avenue, a handful of ice skaters glided under the lights in Pershing Park.

Continuing past the Treasury Building, they cleared the first security checkpoint before proceeding up East Executive Avenue. A fresh layer of unblemished snow blanketed the immaculate grounds of the South Lawn, as if ordered expressly for the evening's festivities. The pillar of effervescent water rising out of the fountain glowed with an internal light.

Egan studied the elegant façade of the White House as they walked and found the scene worthy of a rendering by Currier and Ives. The home of the American President was designed to make an impression, and it did so to great effect. Egan felt a swell of patriotic pride that he was, tonight, an invited guest in a place that was once home to Thomas Jefferson and Abraham Lincoln.

A small fountain in line with the sidewalk marked the east entry to the White House grounds. There, Egan and Niki were cleared by both Secret Service and a representative of the White House Social Office before passing through the wrought iron gate.

"Welcome to the White House," the Secret Service agent said as he returned their credentials.

"Thank you," Egan replied.

They followed another couple along a broad walk to the illuminated colonnade that defined the entry to the East Wing. The covered porch was decorated for the holidays and glowed with the warmth of the festive season.

Through the doors, a uniformed Secret Service officer made a final cursory check of their credentials and then pointed them through a metal detector.

"I think we're finally in," Egan offered as he cleared the magnetometer without a beep. He had been briefed on the security procedures and brought only a photo ID and the key card to his hotel room.

At the coat check, Niki removed her scarf to reveal her black mane coiffed in an up do with a halo of ringlet curls. Egan helped her with her coat and received his first glimpse of the red beaded gown that wrapped Niki's lithe form. Delicate spirals of gold hung from her ears like tinsel and around her neck she wore a braided gold torc. Niki completed her transformation by trading her boots for a chic pair of Manolo Blahniks. In heels, she stood eye to eye with Egan.

"May I escort you to the Residence, ma'am?" a chiseled Marine in full dress uniform asked.

"You may," Niki replied, accepting the young man's offered arm.

The Marine led them down the East Colonnade. The windows were adorned with large magnolia wreaths dressed in red and framed with green boxwood garlands, beyond which lay the Kennedy Garden under a blanket of snow. The colonnade ended at the Visitor's Foyer, where an arch of decorated garland accented a large bronze bust of Lincoln. A pair of large paneled wood doors beneath an ornate elliptical transom stood open, providing access to the central hall that ran the length of the Residence's Ground Floor.

The polished marble on the walls glistened and a series of intersecting vaults ran the length of the broad corridor. Barely a third of the way down the hall, the Marine guided them up a long marble staircase, at the top of which Egan caught a glimpse of the East Room to his right.

They turned left into the Entrance Hall, and then up the Grand Stair to the second floor, arriving at the Yellow Oval Room.

"This is where the President and the First Lady will host the reception," the Marine said as they reached the door. "I hope you enjoy the evening."

"Thank you," both Egan and Niki replied.

As the Marine withdrew, he gave Egan an approving smile, then performed a perfect about-face and headed back toward the stair.

"I have to thank you again for asking me to accompany you," Niki said as they entered the Yellow Oval, her voice barely above a whisper.

"You deserve a better seat to this particular event than in the press pool. And based on the looks you're getting, I should be the one thanking you."

A White House photographer documented their arrival at the reception. Inside, dozens of couples milled about. Some faces Egan recognized, but most were unknown to him. A beautifully decorated twelve-foot tree stood on the opposite side of the oval, flanked by two windows decorated with wreathes.

"What are you thinking about?" Niki asked.

"Maggie was always better at social events than me. She would have really enjoyed this. My being here is a fitting tribute to her life's work."

"May I offer you a drink?" a server asked.

Niki requested a white wine, Egan a cranberry juice over ice.

As the server withdrew, the President and the First Lady appeared in the doorway. She was draped in golden silk brocade, the delicate fabric shimmering in the light. The President, known for his cool demeanor, wore his tailored tuxedo as comfortably as James Bond.

"Good evening," the President said warmly—all conversation in the room stopped. "My wife and I are thrilled that you could join us tonight to honor President and Mrs. Mensah of Dutannuru. Our guests will arrive soon, and we will join you shortly. In the meantime, enjoy."

The First Couple nodded to a few friends, then turned and swept away.

"Did you see that dress?" Niki asked softly. "I might as well be wearing a paper bag."

"It's rude to outshine a bride at her wedding," Egan chided, "and equally rude to do so to our hostess on such an important occasion. But as elegant and attractive a woman as the First Lady is, she can only dream of wearing a dress the way you do."

Niki blushed and dropped her gaze with a bemused smile.

"I could never—"

"Niki," Egan said, cutting her off. "The only polite response to a compliment is *thank you*."

"Thank you."

"You're welcome."

After their drinks arrived, a couple broke away from a group of guests near the tree and moved toward them. The man looked to be in his early forties, thin and wiry with a hatchet face of sharp, angular planes. The woman on his arm was an attractive brunette, well into her second trimester.

"Ross Egan?" the man asked.

Egan nodded and offered his hand. "And you're Daniel Page. A pleasure to meet you."

Page accepted Egan's hand in a firm, boney, grip. "The pleasure is mine. It's an honor to meet a recipient of the Nobel Peace Prize."

"Once the President and the guest of honor arrive, the place will be thick with them."

"Indeed," Page chuckled. "And this is my wife, Elena."

"Delighted to meet you," Elena said with genuine warmth. "What you did in Dutannuru was quite simply amazing."

"Thank you," Egan replied, shooting a quick glance at Niki. "And I assume you saw the photograph of that famous night."

"Why yes."

"My guest is the photographer," Egan said proudly. "May I introduce Niki Adashi."

"You were there?" Elena asked, amazed.

"Yes," Niki replied.

"Oh my," Elena gasped, her free hand shooting to her abdomen.

"Another kick?" Page asked.

Elena nodded. "This child is a gymnast, I swear. Would you mind sitting on the couch with me for a moment? I have about a million questions to ask you, but I simply *must* get off my feet."

"Of course," Niki replied.

Arm in arm, the two women moved to one of the finely upholstered sofas.

"I won't let my wife monopolize your guest," Page promised.

"Judging by the other ladies gathering around them, I think she might be the perfect icebreaker."

"I have to admit, I'm surprised you know who I am. Are you into politics?"

"Not really, but I have a friend who is, and she made up a set of flash cards so I'd know who's who. If I remember your card correctly, you managed the President's last campaign and even wrote a book about it. So, I guess we have that in common."

"You ran a presidential campaign?" Page joked.

"God no. I cowrote a book with President Mensah. It's coming out after the first of the year."

"Then you'll be hitting the promotional trail about the time we start campaigning in earnest." Page sipped his drink, his flinty eyes still locked on Egan.

"Our schedule looks brutal, but it's only for a few months. Then I can slip back into obscurity. I can't imagine the gauntlet you and your boss have to run through until November."

"We should have the nomination sewn up before my next child is born," Page said confidently. "Then we'll get a bit of a breather before the convention and fall campaign."

"You don't think Governor Lynn will give you a run for your money?"

"I thought you weren't into politics."

"I'm not," Egan replied, "other than to educate myself on who the candidates on my ballot are and their views on key issues. I take voting seriously."

Page tapped his glass to Egan's. "Here's to an educated voting public."

Both men took a sip to complete the toast.

"Regarding the governor of the great state of Pennsylvania, I think an intraparty challenge to a sitting president is a suicide mission."

"She must think the President is vulnerable if she's willing to take a shot."

"That, and she'll be four years older next time around, and running against a field of young up-and-comers. In the governor's mind, it's now or never. I admire her nerve, but her campaign is quixotic."

Egan chuckled.

"What's so funny?" Page asked.

"As a guy who knows a little about windmills, I find the thought of tilting at them amusing," Egan explained. "My father owns a wind farm in Michigan."

"I see. And as I recall, your field of expertise is electrical power?"

"Yes."

"Given that and your notoriety over that business in Dutannuru, I'd wager that you would be a more formidable opponent than Governor Lynn."

"Then it's a good thing I'm not running."

"Good for the President. Another thing that would be good for the President is your endorsement."

Egan shook his head in disbelief. "You're joking."

"I'm a campaign manager. I never joke about contributions and endorsements. You're a hot commodity, so your endorsement translates into votes."

"But I don't belong to any party," Egan said.

"All the better," Page countered. "Independents will decide this election."

"Fame is a poor substitute for making an educated decision. The President has a record to run on and the voting public should decide to retain him based on that and not the endorsement of an actress or a rock star. I won't shill for any politician, but I will give every candidate, including the President, my fair consideration and make my decision privately."

Page studied Egan carefully for a moment, and then nodded.

"I respect that, but I had to ask. You don't seem at all pleased with the notoriety that comes with winning a Nobel Prize."

"If I'd won a Nobel for having discovered something that benefited mankind, that would be one thing. The path to peace was shown to us two thousand years ago, and it remains the road less traveled. All Mensah and I did was transplant a shoot from the American tree of Liberty, in Africa."

"No small feat."

"Perhaps, but the prize really belongs to the people of Dutannuru for seizing peace out of war. The real demonstration of that comes in a couple of weeks."

"Oh?" Page asked.

"I've heard it said that the only job better than president is ex-president. Mensah is popular enough that if he wanted the job for another term, the legislature would have offered an amendment to the people and changed the constitution on presidential term limits. Like George Washington, he sees the importance of holding power for only so long. The beauty of our system is that we peacefully create ex-presidents."

"Not too soon, I hope," Page said wryly. "Otherwise, I'm out of a job. Speaking of jobs, we do have one that might be of interest you. Would you consider being our next ambassador to Dutannuru?"

"Is Quimby stepping down?"

"No, but there's another post opening up unexpectedly and we're thinking of shifting her there. You'd be a perfect fit for Dutannuru and I see no problem getting you through the confirmation process."

"I'm committed through the first half of next year, but my publisher would shoot me if I didn't consider your offer seriously. It's the kind of publicity I think she'd kill for."

"It wouldn't hurt us, either. We're looking at making the shift in late spring, but I would appreciate it if you would keep this between us for now. I'll let the President know that you are open to the idea."

"Fair enough."

The President and the First Lady returned to the Yellow Oval with the guests of honor and their entourage. Page excused himself and joined his wife, and Niki returned to Egan.

Instead of a formal receiving line, the two presidential couples made a slow circuit of the room, with the hosts making the introductions. Egan and Niki held their place, waiting their turn.

"Is this not exciting? We are going to meet the President," Niki said in a low voice.

"We've already met Mensah," Egan replied.

"Not him, the President of the United States," Niki said with the pride of a recently naturalized citizen.

As the two presidential couples moved toward them, Egan caught the President sharing a quick glance with his campaign manager. Page gave an almost imperceptible nod of his head.

"These two, I believe I should introduce to you," Mensah announced to the President and the First Lady. "It is with great pleasure that I present Ms. Niki Adashi, a daughter of Dutannuru and a fine photographer who has recently won the Pulitzer Prize for her work in my country."

"Ms. Adashi, my wife and I are delighted that you could be with us tonight," the President said warmly.

"Thank you, Mr. President," Niki replied breathlessly. "Madam, everything is just beautiful, and your dress is simply stunning."

"The White House Staff is amazing," the First Lady agreed. "As for my dress, I honestly think Marcia Amagansett could make a sack of potatoes in a dress look divine."

"Dear, you are no sack of potatoes," the President chided affectionately.

"And this," Mensah continued, "is a very good friend to me, and to all the people of Dutannuru—Ross Egan."

"Your reputation precedes you," the President said as he extended his hand. "I am truly honored to have you here with us tonight."

A White House photographer captured the meeting between three recent winners of the Nobel Peace Prize.

"Thank you for inviting me here to honor my friend. This is a unique privilege." Egan then turned to the First Lady. "The graciousness of a house is a reflection of the people who make it their home. Thank you for your hospitality."

"You're welcome," the First Lady said with a soft smile. "I hope you both enjoy the evening."

★

THE RECEPTION IN THE Yellow Oval continued for another forty-five minutes, then the guests were ushered down the stairs into the Entrance Hall, where the majority of those invited to the state dinner waited. Egan and Niki crossed the marble floor, a checkerboard of light and dark polished stone, and found a spot to stand along the colonnade.

After a few moments, the President, his wife, and the guests of honor descended the Grand Staircase. The United States Marine Band played four "Ruffles and Flourishes" followed by "Hail to the Chief" and the national anthems of Dutannuru and the United States.

After all the guests had filed through a formal receiving line, the two presidential couples walked down the Cross Hall to the State Dining Room, which was exquisitely decorated for the holiday season. Both presidents spoke briefly as the guests enjoyed a five-course meal that would have earned any restaurant a James Beard Foundation Award.

"I wish I had not worn so tight a dress," Niki moaned as the dessert plates were cleared away and the guests moved on to the opulent East Room for the evening's entertainment.

"The great thing about tuxedos is they have these fasteners on the waist that allow you to loosen them a bit."

"You men are very fortunate indeed."

"I thank the Good Lord and my father for my Y-chromosome each and every day."

As they stepped into the East Room, Egan was immediately struck by the size of the space. It was larger than any place he had called home. Fresh garlands with blue hydrangea and eucalyptus accented the four fireplaces in the room, which had magnificently decorated fir trees standing at each end.

Seating for all the guests was arranged in a semicircle around an area that contained an array of traditional and electronic instruments. Once the guests were seated, the President moved to center stage.

"The musicians who will entertain us tonight," the President began, "have been the joyful stewards of the modern soundtrack of the Christmas season for many years. I am very pleased to present Mannheim Steamroller."

"I enjoy this group very much," Niki said as the musicians appeared from the adjacent Green Room and took the stage. "Maggie played them for me during her first Christmas in my village."

Mannheim Steamroller performed an hour-long set of seasonal music in their uniquely elegant style, culminating in their stirring rendition of "Stille Nacht."

The musicians took their bows to an audience that included some of the nation's most powerful people, all on their feet applauding the outstanding performance. And as they clapped, several members of the audience felt their cell phones vibrating in their pockets. Others rushed to quell their contribution to a cacophony of disparate ring tones.

"What's happening?" the President tersely asked his campaign manager, alarmed that a situation might be emerging somewhere.

"I don't know," Page replied as he fumbled with his phone.

Egan watched as Niki fished a thin handset out of her clutch purse. Having left his phone at the hotel, he was one of the few people in the room not trying to quell a buzzing or chiming gadget.

"This message is very strange," Niki said, puzzled, as she read the luminous screen.

"You got an odd text, too?" a Texan in a tuxedo asked, his brow furrowed as he read the message on his iPhone.

Niki nodded. "I have never received one without a sender's name or a phone number."

The Texan glanced over Niki's shoulder. "I got the same damn thing."

"What's it say?" Egan asked.

Niki turned her phone toward him. It read: **Who Is I?**

# 7

TWO ARCTIC CAT SNOWMOBILES cruised across the frozen lake—a gray-white slab of solid ice ten times the size of Manhattan. An early freeze roared out of Canada in a series of blasts that sealed the vast lake completely by Thanksgiving weekend. Six weeks of polar temperatures had thickened the ice to eighteen inches at mid-lake and the winter fishing season was in full swing.

Mike Unden rode beside his father, Jacob, toward a cluster of shanties out on the lake. The structures ranged from simple wooden sheds to elaborate constructions outfitted with all the amenities. A mix of pickup trucks, SUVs, and snowmobiles were parked chaotically on the ice as several fishermen set up beside one of the larger shanties for a bowl game tailgate party.

Mike eased back on the throttle, slowing his sled to a crawl as they neared his father's unusual shanty. Inspired by a visit to Disney's Epcot, the old farmer had built a small geodesic dome with an elongated airlock entry that he called his igloo. The entire structure could be easily broken down by two people with a ladder and a ratchet wrench and fit in back of a trailer pulled by Jacob's F-150.

Once assembled, the igloo was anchored to the ice to keep it from blowing away in the gusts that roared across the lake. A small satellite dish mounted atop the dome hinted at the simple comforts hidden inside.

Both men parked their sleds and dismounted, the elder a tad slower than his son.

"How you doing, Pa?" Mike asked.

"Little stiff, but a bad day of fishing beats a great day of work."

"So I've heard. Let me help you with the cooler."

Mike unwound the bungee cords holding a large rectangular cooler to the back of his father's Bearcat Z1 XT. The utility sled was a steady draft horse compared with the thoroughbred that was Mike's CFR 1000, but both men shared a passion for their winter mounts.

As Mike hefted the cooler, his father unlocked the igloo's outer door and they stepped into the dome. The bright morning sun shone through triangular windows, warming and illuminating the interior. The shanty floor, like the rest of the dome, was made from insulated panels that sealed the structure tight.

"How's the hole?" Mike asked as he set the cooler beside a bench that served as the igloo's kitchen counter.

Jacob opened a hinged door in the floor to reveal the lake below. Several inches of new ice covered the top of a hole in the center of the exposed frozen lake.

"Needs a reaming."

"On it."

Mike grabbed a six-inch offset auger and quickly reopened the hole in the ice. As his father unloaded bait from the cooler, Mike dragged a small generator and propane tank out of the igloo. Just to the left of the entry, he plugged the generator into an electrical box and connected the propane tank to a quick-disconnect gas line. He pulled the starter cord, bringing the four-stroke engine rumbling to life. Satisfied, he returned inside.

"You got power for the TV and the heater's ready to go."

Mike slipped off a glove, picked up the remote, and flipped through the channels. It was too early for the pregame shows, so he stopped on a documentary about the Vietnam War.

"You wanna watch this?"

Jacob glanced at the screen and shook his head. "Saw enough when I was there. See if you can find me a western."

Skimming through the satellite guide, Mike settled on *The Treasure of the Sierra Madre.*

" 'Badges? We don't need no stinking badges!' " Mike quoted in a poor imitation of the infamous bandito.

"Don't quit your day job," Jacob opined as he looked over his fishing lures.

Mike turned on the small propane heater and set the temperature. It wasn't enough to turn the igloo into a sauna, but it would keep his father comfortable. That was the trick with his father's condition. Jacob Unden was a tough old bird—just not as tough as he once was.

"Better get going if you want to get your ride in before the game."

"Yeah, yeah." Mike tugged his gloves back on. "Call me if you need anything."

"Like you can hear me over your sled."

"Love you, Pa," Mike said as he headed out the door.

Jacob paused and waited for the sound of his son's snowmobile. He heard the muffled thunder of the engine, the shift in pitch and volume as the sled quickly raced away.

"I love you, too, son."

Jacob settled on a lure, tied his line, and baited the hook. The igloo had all the comforts of home, including a battered La-Z-Boy chair whose cushions fit Jacob's body like a glove. Mounted to the floor beside the chair stood a rod holder. He dropped his line into the hole and set his rod.

Too early to justify a beer, he poured a cup of black coffee from a Thermos and surveyed his tiny refuge. He enjoyed many fond memories of this place, including, he smiled, the conception of his son one January morning when the fish just weren't biting.

He walked over to the heater and warmed himself. Outside, a wispy trail of smoke rose out of the exhaust vent. Jacob set his coffee cup down on the counter and pulled a small screwdriver out of his tackle box. He gently loosened the screw on the crimp collar that held the heater's flexible exhaust pipe in place by a half turn and slid the end of the pipe back. Immediately, he felt the hot exhaust leaking through the gap. Jacob put the screwdriver away, picked up his coffee cup, and settled into his chair.

★

AROUND NOON, MIKE UNDEN drove his sled up to the igloo and parked. He'd enjoyed a great ride both on the trails and racing across open stretches of the lake. It was cold, but the wind was light under a perfectly blue Dakota sky. He slipped off his helmet and opened the outer door.

"Hope you got that chili simmering, Pa, 'cause I'm hungry."

Mike did not smell the tangy aroma of his father's four-alarm chili as he entered the igloo. In fact, he smelled nothing at all. His father sat slumped in his chair, head back, lifeless. Shards of a broken coffee cup lay on the plywood floor.

Almost immediately, Mike felt he was having trouble breathing. His head spinning, he lunged back through the doors outside and drew in as much fresh air as his lungs could hold. After his mind cleared, he disconnected the propane tank to kill the heater. Then he dialed 911.

# 8

ROSS EGAN SAT BENEATH a poolside pergola staring out at the Atlantic Ocean. Though it was a cool night by Florida standards and cold compared to Dutannuru, he sat comfortably in a pair of khakis and a golf shirt with a pullover windbreaker. In one hand, he swirled a fine California Syrah in a broad-bowled wineglass while the other held an exquisite Ramon Allones Gigante Double Corona. Modest waves crashed ashore in a predictable, soothing rhythm.

"...and if he stays healthy, the Packers could make it to the Super Bowl," Leon Egan opined. "Isn't that right, son?"

"Uh, yeah," Ross replied, drawn out of his thoughts to answer his father.

"That's a stirring vote of confidence," conservative talk radio host Garr Denby shot back as he flicked a long ash off the end of his cigar. He then turned to their host. "What do you think?"

"The Pack has played well all year," Burton Randell conceded, "but they had a relatively easy schedule. Carolina dropped a couple more games, but when they lost, it was either in the final seconds of regulation or in OT, and against a quality opponent. Any of those games could have gone their way. The Panthers are the most dangerous wild-card team I've seen in years."

Following an evening of good food and college bowl games, the gentlemanly quartet had retreated to the pergola to enjoy the waning hours of the year with good wine and cigars. To the west stood the Florida retreat of Maya Randell and her husband. The Raffles Hotel in Singapore, where the Randells enjoyed their twenty-fifth anniversary, served as the architectural inspiration for the colonial-style villa.

Egan was there with his parents, Leon and Rhetta, who wintered in a condominium just up the coast, near Vero Beach. The Randells' twin daughters were in Palm Beach with their husbands celebrating the arrival of the new year, their young children left in the capable hands of their doting grandparents.

Ross's cell phone buzzed like an angry hornet. He glanced at the screen and smiled before he answered.

"Yes, Mr. President."

Mensah's hearty laugh poured through the receiver. "You only have about seven more hours to say that. Then I will just be another old man in Dutannuru. I am calling to wish you a most happy New Year, my friend."

"And to you, as well. I was just thinking about you. How are things in the capital?"

"The new year arrived five hours ago, and the celebration shows no sign of abating. I think it will just flow into today's inaugural celebration."

"The people of Dutannuru have much to celebrate, not the least of which is your years of good stewardship. Today is the first time they've greeted a new year without the threat of war."

"Yes, this is a happy day," Mensah said. "But also a busy one for me."

"I appreciate your call and I look forward to spending time with you after your return to private life."

"That will be good. I must go now, but I will see you soon."

"Can't wait," Ross replied.

"If only it was *our* president," Denby remarked sarcastically as Ross pocketed his phone. "I'd be out celebrating in the streets if I thought his last hours in office were ticking away."

"You've got another year before that happens," Burton said, "and only if most of the voters feel as you do."

"Gallup and Rasmussen seem to think so, and my Arbitron numbers have never been higher," Denby offered. "The mood of conservatives across the country is absolutely electric. The only problem is there's no Reagan to galvanize it." Denby turned to Egan. "Or somebody like your pal Mensah."

"I can guess how you feel about the President and Governor Lynn," Ross said, "but what about the six Republicans?"

"Vegas is having an easier time picking the Super Bowl winner than figuring the GOP nominee," Denby replied. "There are two governors, an old senator, a quirky congresswoman, a four-star general, and a media billionaire. Any of 'em would be better than what we got now, but no one is a clear favorite. I read your book, and *you* would stand as good a chance as any of them, and better than most after what you did in Africa."

Maya stepped out onto the terrace and glided toward the four men.

"The management of Raffles Palm Beach is sorry to inform you gentlemen that it is closing time at the Winston Churchill Bar," she announced. "So if you are quite through discussing the state of the British Empire, it's time to stub out those nasty cigars and come inside. The ball drops in five minutes."

In response, the quartet each took a final draw on their cigars and lofted four perfect rings of smoke into the air.

" 'A woman is only a woman,' " Burton offered, " 'but a cigar is a smoke.' "

"You can quote Kipling all you like," Maya shot back at her husband, "but you better not have smoky lips if you expect to get some sugar at midnight."

Burton looked at his wife and the remnant of the Corona in his fingertips, and stubbed the cigar out.

✯

HOMER HOPPS STOOD IN front of a large flat-screen television watching a band he could not name play live from an outdoor stage near New York's Times Square. He tried to keep an open mind with regard to music but some trends in popular culture simply eluded him. He was the only person in the windowless meeting room watching the celebration. Deb McColl and the rest of her rogue programmers sat glued to laptops and workstations, young men and women fueled on energy drinks and salty junk food.

"Go or no go time, people," Hopps announced. "Con Ed?"

"Go," a twenty-two-year-old Cal Tech grad replied.

"EMS?"

"Go," another rogue answered.

"Network feeds?"

"Go."

"Package?"

McColl looked up from her screen at Hopps. "Go."

A devilish smile curled the ends of Hopps's mouth. "All systems are go. On my mark, we are T-minus two minutes. And...mark."

★

"WHERE ARE THE KIDS?" Leon asked as he sat on the couch beside his wife.

"Camped out in the playroom. They held on as long as they could," Rhetta explained, "but the last one nodded off about forty minutes ago."

They gathered in the den, an immense flat screen displaying the scene in Times Square. Despite the cold, a record crowd filled Broadway and the intersecting streets in the great annual tradition.

"Ross, would you do the honors?" Maya asked as she handed out noisemakers.

"My pleasure."

Ross gently twisted the cork from a bottle of Roederer Estate Brut and felt it release with a soft pop. He then filled six champagne flutes with the effervescent liquid and distributed them.

"The ball's dropping!" Rhetta said excitedly. "I love this part."

"...five...four...three...two...one..." they counted down with the crowd in New York City.

At the stroke of midnight, Times Square went dark. The celebratory shout died in its first syllable as the mood shifted from joy to confusion.

"What the hell," the host of the program exclaimed before the network cut his microphone feed.

Television cameras powered by stand-alone generators continued to broadcast the eerie scene of a packed Times Square plunged into darkness. Celebrants wearing illuminated necklaces and deely bobbers appeared like tiny fireflies flickering in the shadow.

Calls from police officers to remain calm could be heard over the murmuring crowd.

"I hope this isn't..." Rhetta said, her voice quavering.

"Power's gone out, dear," Leon reassured his wife. "That's all."

The first seconds of the new year passed like an eternity. There was no panic, no sudden rush to flee the darkness, just a stillness of anticipation.

The people in Times Square were waiting for a sign. And then it came.

It started with the jumbotron screens that covered the Times building, then spread from screen to screen. A cryptic message: WHO IS I?

"My God," Denby roared. "It's a college prank. Probably one of those egghead schools, like Stanford or MIT. No offense."

"None taken," Maya replied.

Burton set his champagne flute down on the bar and checked an incoming message on his cell phone.

"But what does it mean?" Rhetta asked.

"It means those brainy engineers flunked freshman English," Denby answered sardonically.

The conservative talk show host's sharp humor was a clear sign of his relief that a tragic event was not unfolding. Instead, the Times Square blackout would provide a rich vein of humor for his next broadcast.

The surreal scene continued for another thirty seconds before the messages disappeared. Then the lights of Times Square blared back on to full intensity and the LED illuminated ball completed its descent. Fireworks erupted from the rooftop and the celebration, somewhat subdued, resumed.

"Whoever's responsible for that stunt ought to be strung up," Leon grumbled. "The memory of 9/11 is still too fresh for the folks in New York. Like when those idiots flew Air Force One low over the city just to take a picture of it."

"They blew what could have been a perfect PR moment," Denby agreed. "Most of the people in New York City voted for the President, and his ham-handed staff goes and scares them half to death. If they'd gone public, they would have had thousands of people out cheering as the plane flew over."

"Regardless of whoever is responsible for this little shenanigan," Maya announced, "this is still the start of a new year. You all have my best wishes for one filled with love, family, and happiness."

"Hear, hear," Denby seconded.

"Bravo," Maya whispered into her husband's ear. "Please extend my congratulations and continued good wishes for the new year to our team."

"Already done," Burton replied proudly. "And I'm sure they're not waiting another two hours to pop the corks in Montana."

Champagne glasses clinked and a round of kisses and embraces were exchanged. Maya saved Ross for last and approached him with a mix of expectation and concern.

"Happy New Year," Ross said as he embraced her.

Maya kissed him on the cheek and then whispered in his ear.

"Last year was a good one for you, and God knows you deserved it. May this year bring with it all that we hope."

"Amen to that," Ross replied softly.

Maya gave Ross a tight squeeze before slipping from his embrace and turning toward the others.

"I must beg your indulgence for a moment. Now that it is officially the new year, Ross and I must attend to a small business matter. We will return to you shortly. For those who feel the need for something sweet, I whipped up a decadent chocolate mousse that's in the refrigerator."

"*Decadent* is the operative word here," Burton agreed as he pulled a tray of chilled glass vessels containing a dark frothy substance topped with a raspberry. "Maya makes it from her grandmother's recipe and a whole mess of dark chocolate went into this."

"I'll bet it pairs nicely with the brut," Denby speculated.

"You'd win that bet," Maya replied. "Now save us some. We'll be right back."

MAYA LED ROSS TO A small room on the north end of the villa. Three sides of the room featured large arch windows that, in daylight, overlooked a colorful garden. It had bamboo plank flooring and a ceiling paneled in painted beadboard. The plaster walls and wood trim were finished in off-white and pastel hues. What could have easily been a sunroom retreat was instead the home office from which Maya and her husband managed their business empire.

Ross sat on a white wicker sofa as Maya retrieved a thick leather folio from a locked desk drawer. She sat beside him and carefully laid out a set of bound contracts on the glass-topped coffee table. Beside the contracts, she set a pair of fountain pens made from wood taken from the original US Navy frigate USS *Constitution*.

"So, this is it," Ross said.

Maya nodded. "The birth of Terrafuma Energy. All your years of research, your life's work, have led to this moment. A moment that will change the world."

He leaned forward and studied the cover of the contract. It bore the logo of a company that would exist as soon as he and Maya added their signatures to these documents. While the paperwork before them was thick with legal boilerplate, the essence of the agreement was simple. For his part, Ross would invest Terrafuma with his intellectual property—a permanent license on the revolutionary technologies that he created. Maya would provide the considerable financial resources required to establish this new private company. They were equal shareholders in this venture, a dream they both had nurtured over the long years of research and development.

"There are only two things I can think of that I was more excited to sign," Ross said. "My wedding license, and my first driver's license."

"Only one was worth more," Maya opined.

Ross removed the cap from one of the pens and flipped to the tabbed signature page. Slowly, he guided the pen through the loops and curves of his name. Maya then added her signature to consummate the deal.

They completed the remaining copies quickly and Maya returned all but Ross's copy to her locked drawer.

"So, now it's official," Maya declared as she returned to the sofa. "You are the first billionaire of the new year. On behalf of those of us who have created something worthy of earning three significant commas of net worth, I welcome you to the club."

Ross shook his head and smiled. "Thank you."

"Now before we can celebrate, we must attend to Terrafuma's first client."

Maya tapped a few keystrokes into a handheld remote to activate a secure teleconferencing program. A moment later, a flat-screen wall monitor glowed with a view into a room half a world away. Looking back at them was an Asian man with a round face and graying black hair. It was Chen Yung-Chin, leader of the Standing Committee of the National People's Congress—a position of power second only to the Chinese presidency.

"Good day, Chairman Chen," Maya said with a polite nod of her head.

"And to you, Ms. Randell," Chen replied.

"It is my great pleasure to at last introduce to you my associate, Ross Egan."

"I am delighted to finally make your acquaintance," Chen said. "We share a similar background in electrical engineering. Speaking as one engineer to another, your work is most revolutionary."

"Thank you," Ross replied.

"I trust that your review team was satisfied with our demonstration at the Dongjaio Power Plant?" Maya asked.

"Indeed. Their only disappointment was in not seeing how your innovation was accomplished."

"Will respect for our intellectual property be an issue?" Egan asked.

"It will not," Chen vowed. "Separate installations will be provided as defined in the contract. All activity within those installations will be the sole responsibility of Terrafuma Energy."

"And the payment terms we proposed?" Maya asked.

"Most unusual," Chen replied, his eyes narrowing, "but what you offer is also most unusual. China's investment in US Treasuries has lost considerable value due to actions taken by your President and his most significant supporter. Paying Terrafuma in Treasuries is agreeable assuming that you can meet the timeline."

"Our project team is ready to scale up the work at Dongjaio as soon as the contracts are signed," Maya said. "From there, they will move on to your other power generation facilities."

"Then I suggest you make arrangements for that work to commence as soon as possible. I will sign the contracts upon the conclusion of this call," Chen promised. "The first transfer will be made into Terrafuma's account at the open of business tomorrow."

"And the other matter we discussed?" Maya asked.

"Ah, the *favor*," Chen said, smiling conspiratorially. "Consider our warming interest in joining the President's New York Climate Exchange an act of gratitude from the People's Republic of China."

"We look forward to the fruits of those discussions," Maya said with a polite nod of her head.

"Until we speak again." Chen returned the nod, and then terminated the call.

Ross turned to Maya. "That went well."

"And the President will be thrilled with the prospect of China joining his climate exchange. A diplomatic and environmental coup—it's the kind of accomplishment that may help him win the election."

"It'll certainly do something to his chances in the fall," Ross agreed.

"Yes, but first we must help him through the primaries. Four years ago, Governor Lynn lost her party's nomination by the slimmest of margins, and there are many who now regret their decision to back the President. She presents a formidable challenge for the nomination."

"And serious contenders draw the big money."

"They do indeed," Maya said. "And as my dissatisfaction with the President is known in certain circles, the governor and I have an area of common interest."

"When do you meet?" Ross asked.

"In a few days. And instead of a campaign contribution, I'll make Governor Lynn and her husband an offer she can't refuse."

Made in the USA
Charleston, SC
10 November 2012